'I nodded "yes, yes" as I read the stories collected from women, like me, who are childless by circumstance. With candor, they articulate the self-blame, social isolation, layers of intangible losses and indescribable grief we experience. Finally, we are no longer alone.'

– *Kathleen Guthrie Woods, Life Without Baby columnist and author of* The Mother of All Dilemmas *of related interest*

The Forgiveness Project
Stories for a Vengeful Age
Marina Cantacuzino
Forewords by Archbishop Emeritus Desmond Tutu and Alexander McCall Smith
ISBN 978 1 84905 566 6 (hardback)
ISBN 978 1 78592 000 4 (paperback)
eISBN 978 1 78450 006 1

Forgiveness is Really Strange
Masi Noor and Marina Cantacuzino
Art by Sophie Standing
ISBN 978 1 78592 124 7
eISBN 978 0 85701 279 1

Anxiety is Really Strange
Steve Haines
Art by Sophie Standing
ISBN 978 1 84819 407 6 (hardback)
ISBN 978 1 84819 389 5 (paperback)
eISBN 978 0 85701 345 3

Take It as a Compliment
Maria Stoian
ISBN 978 1 84905 697 7
eISBN 978 0 85701 242 5

MOTHERHOOD
MISSED

*Stories from Women Who Are
Childless by Circumstance*

Lois Tonkin
Foreword by Jody Day

Jessica Kingsley *Publishers*
London and Philadelphia

First published in 2019
by Jessica Kingsley Publishers
73 Collier Street
London N1 9BE, UK
and
400 Market Street, Suite 400
Philadelphia, PA 19106, USA

www.jkp.com

Library of Congress Cataloging in Publication Data
A CIP catalog record for this book is available from the Library of Congress

British Library Cataloguing in Publication Data
A CIP catalogue record for this book is available from the British Library

ISBN 978 1 78592 337 1
eISBN 978 1 78450 659 9

Printed and bound in the United States

For Addie, Dexter, Lachlan and Tara

Contents

Foreword by Jody Day   **9**

Acknowledgements   **19**

Introduction   **21**

Gina, 43, Lives in the US   **30**

Toni, 46, Lives in New Zealand   **36**

Andrea, 47, Lives in England   **41**

Lynne, 39, Lives in New Zealand   **46**

Molly, 44, Lives in New Zealand   **52**

Leeann, 42, Lives in Australia   **57**

Bron, 38, Lives in New Zealand   **64**

Persephone, 44, Lives in England   **69**

Sonja, 55, Lives in New Zealand   **75**

Claudia, 35, Lives in Australia   **82**

Louise, 40, Lives in New Zealand   **87**

Hannah, 45, Lives in Spain — 91

Maree, 33, Lives in New Zealand — 98

Julia, 48, Lives in New Zealand — 102

Raewyn, 47, Lives in India — 108

Genevieve, 45, Lives in England — 117

Holly, 36, Lives in New Zealand — 123

Bridget, 43, Lives in New Zealand — 128

Yvonne, 46, Lives in England — 134

Deborah, 45, Lives in New Zealand — 140

Brigitte, 40, Lives in England — 145

Georgina, 49, Lives in New Zealand — 150

Rebecca, 48, Lives in Australia — 156

Rachael, 46, Lives in New Zealand — 162

Teena, 47, Lives in New Zealand — 168

Rose, 41, Lives in New Zealand — 174

Shanti, 46, Lives in England — 178

Shelley, 50, Lives in New Zealand — 184

Kathryn, 45, Lives in New Zealand — 190

Stella, 57, Lives in New Zealand — 196

Vicki, 44, Lives in New Zealand — 203

Natasha, 55, Lives in England — 208

About the Author — 217

Index — 218

Foreword

It is an honour to write the foreword for what I believe is a very important book. It is the first time that so many personal testimonies to one of the biggest untold stories of our generation are gathered together – the stories of women who are childless by circumstance.

I first came across Lois Tonkin's work exploring the disenfranchised grief of childless women in her doctoral thesis and I referenced it in the second edition of my book – *Living the Life Unexpected: 12 Weeks to Your Plan B for a Meaningful and Fulfilling Future Without Children* – published in 2016. It turns out that on the other side of the world, she was paying close attention to my work too, and it was with delightful mutual recognition that we found ourselves sitting next to each other at the first FertilityFest.com in the UK in 2016, as I was waiting to go up and give my talk. We struck up both a friendship and a professional collaboration and I trusted her with introductions to some of the women whose stories you are about to read.

When I published my first blog for Gateway Women back in April 2011, I had no idea what a huge taboo I was breaking by being open about my situation. I used my real name, my real photo and told my real story. And women from all over the world wrote back and said, 'me too'. There didn't even seem to be a language yet to describe the situation that so many childless women found themselves in, of being childless not by choice, yet not really having ever felt that they'd had a clear 'choice' in the matter. I would refer to it initially as, 'a rock and a hard place choice'.

When so many of us are told, aggressively and unhelpfully, by others who fail to appreciate the complexity of the context of those hard choices, 'Yes, you *did* make a choice, you could have had a baby if you'd tried harder/adopted/had a baby on your own', and so on, it's hard to come back from that and decide that this person is offering a safe space to lay out the full picture; to say, 'Spend half an hour listening to this, and see if *you* can really see better choices I could have made at each point, with the knowledge and resources that were available to me at the time.' And of course, in this case, a 'better' choice is always one that is implied to be the one that leads to motherhood. Being childless, whether by choice or not, is still seen as a deviant feminine identity and one to be avoided at all costs. This is the powerful conditioning of the unquestioned and often unseen pronatalist ideology that runs through all our thinking and judgments about motherhood and non-motherhood.

It became clear to me early on that medical infertility was

definitely *not* the whole story behind the largest increase in involuntary childlessness in the UK since the generation of 'surplus women' (as they were known in Britain) born around 1900 and impacted by the loss of so many young men's lives in the First World War and the economic and social difficulties of the Great Depression. In my own writing, the term 'childless by circumstance' arose spontaneously in response to the many stories I was hearing from readers of my blog and, in time, from those women who joined the Gateway Women private online community and attended the groups and workshops I created. However, it would appear to have first been used in print by the Australian academic and author, Leslie Cannold.[1] Another term, 'social infertility', has arisen too (and is now included in the World Health Organization's definition of 'infertility')[2] but that refers more narrowly to the experience of not having a partner to have children with. Childless by circumstance is a systemic term, and this is a systemic issue.

Something that I've noticed since I first started reading and contributing to the media around the issues of childlessness is that gradually the narrative has changed, and it's still evolving. Whereas at first the reporting was mostly about childfree by choice women and how shocking and wonderful their lives were, gradually the stories of women who had tried to have a family using fertility treatments and had failed were starting

---

1   http://cannold.com/articles/article/what-no-baby

2   www.telegraph.co.uk/news/2016/10/19/single-men-will-get-the-right-to-start-a-family-under-new-defini

to appear. The childfree women were painted as exciting and outrageous, with lots of money, wonderful figures and great careers (but unfeminine, ambitious, and destined to die alone), the childless women as failed women, denied the ultimate expression of their femininity, physically and emotionally broken, their lives permanently destroyed. Didn't want – couldn't have: a straightforward dichotomy of the feminine experience and both entirely defined by motherhood. However, the stories of childless by circumstance women were entirely absent, as were (and still are) the stories of women like me who had wanted to become mothers and had found a way to grieve that loss and move forward with their lives in new and personally fulfilling ways.

Yet now, gradually, the grey areas are emerging between (and within) these stories. And the biggest grey area is that of being childless by circumstance. And when I say the biggest, I mean numerically too – Professor Renske Keizer's research coming out of the Netherlands[3] would suggest that 80 per cent of women who don't have children are childless by circumstance, with only 10 per cent childless due to infertility and 10 per cent by choice. This matches my own anecdotal

---

3   The figures come from Professor Renske Keizer's PhD dissertation from Utrecht University (2010): 'Remaining childless: Causes and consequences from a life course perspective'. Her study includes a meta-analysis of childlessness data drawn from the Netherlands and the United States, referred to in this article: www.nwo.nl/actueel/nieuws/2010/Kinderloosheid+is+zelden+een+keuze.html. Keizer is now Full Professor in Family Sociology at Erasmus University, Rotterdam.

experience as someone who has heard many thousands of personal testimonies like the ones Lois shares in this book.

Through my work, I have become the silent vault of so many stories. They have not been mine to share; my role has been to hear them and bear witness to them without closing down the teller with shaming judgments or unhelpful advice. After a morning of such stories in a Gateway Women workshop, I imagine red threads of connection creating a metaphorical cat's cradle across the circle of women: shared experiences of abortion; of successive monogamous partnerships ending without reaching the point of starting a family; of childhood trauma leading to lost decades of potentially fertile womanhood; of partners who already have children and don't want more; of heartbreaking relational wounding by unhappy and narcissistic mothers; of long-term unchosen singleness, dependent siblings, failed adoptions and economic precariousness. In all that time, I haven't met a single 'career woman' or a woman who 'left it too late' (knowingly), and you won't find those in this book either. That's a social trope, like the 'crazy cat lady', and one that entirely misses the systemic context of involuntary childlessness and instead places all the blame (and a huge dollop of shame) on the individual. I see this in how each woman who comes into the workshop feeling alone and shameful about how she 'messed up' her chance at motherhood, leaves having heard other women's stories and, in noticing her own empathy, understanding and appreciation of that complexity, begins to imagine that maybe her story deserves the same. That is the power of testimony.

In 12 Step recovery circles there is an expression that 'you are only as sick as your secrets'[4] and I've come to see how the shame that childless by circumstance women feel has a powerful silencing effect on them, which contributes not only to their own pain and isolation, but also to their ability to heal. Because the social censure of childlessness is a collective process, so the healing from childlessness needs to have a social element too. We need to hear each other's stories to feel supported that the rock-and-a-hard-place choices that we've faced were not because we were stupid or careless, but because human life is complex and choices never happen in a vacuum.

The media, quite naturally, is not the place for a complex unpacking of the systemic issues that the choices of modern women operate within. Time and time again when I've been interviewed by the press, an intelligent journalist has understood this and written a thoughtful paragraph to that effect. And nearly every single time, the editor has removed it, slapped a click-bait headline on it, and left instead the simplistic pronatalist narratives of 'didn't want', 'couldn't have' or, more recently, 'women who left it too late' (to trivialize the experience of childless by circumstance women). Very recently I contributed extensively to a major article for the left-leaning, intellectual British Sunday newspaper *The Observer* on the experience of being a woman without children, by choice or not, on Mother's Day. The journalist and I had in-depth

---

4   www.firststepsrecovery.com/youre-only-as-sick-as-your-secrets

conversations about the social and systemic angles, hardly any of which made it into her final copy. And then when she did submit her commissioned piece, her editor said that she found it too 'gloomy' and asked her to include a story of late motherhood working out 'against the odds'. And I'm sure you can guess which photo the picture editors used to illustrate the whole piece – the mother and baby of course!

So it seems natural that it is in book form that the personal testimonies of women who are childless by circumstance appear. In their own words, and only edited (with their permission) for length and clarity. It is a formidable achievement. Despite the fact that these are stories I hear every day, I have never had an opportunity to hear so many, and in such detail, all in one go. After reading this book I felt that I had lived many other lives, many other stories. I was deeply moved. The stories vary across age, culture, nationality and background but all share a similar theme – that of trying to make sense of the complexity of a modern woman's choices within the confines of an economic and biological reality that isn't always conducive to creating stable, welcoming partnership situations before fertility runs out. I was also very touched to see that a few of them reference the work of Gateway Women as being instrumental to their improved sense of wellbeing.

But why is the path to motherhood so different for 'our' generation? (And by 'our generation', I mean those of us women born in the 1960s and 1970s to mothers who had few, if any, of the opportunities or choices we've had.) I call us 'the shock absorber generation for the sexual revolution'.

In my lifetime (I was born in the UK in 1964) we've had the introduction of the pill (first for married couples, then for unmarried), legalized abortion, women's access to higher education, women's access to the professions and fertility treatments. All in one generation. This has completely changed the dating and mating landscape. We are no longer living in Jane Austen's England and there are other possibilities for women than marriage, menial work or impoverished spinsterhood. In fact, the context of our lived experience as women has probably changed more in my lifetime than at any other point in recorded human history, except perhaps with the shift from matrilineal to patriarchal social structures ten thousand years ago…and that was unlikely to be something that occurred in one generation.

Whereas our mother's generation undoubtedly faced some of the same issues as many of the women in this book – such as the impact of trauma and loss in childhood, the burden of early caring responsibilities, economic disadvantages, unhappy childhoods or a desire to achieve something in the world of work before having children, and so on – it would have been rare for them to have been able to do much about it. Without economic and educational opportunities, without easy and ideologically acceptable access to birth control and abortion, the stories of many of the women in this book would have been as they have been for women for millennia – of early motherhood in less than ideal situations leading perhaps to a lifelong sense of having 'missed out' on personal autonomy and fulfillment. In 1963, Betty Friedan named those women as having 'the problem that has no name'.[5] Now, the daughters and granddaughters of Friedan's generation are wrestling with its opposite – being childless by circumstance and dealing with the personal and societal shame, isolation and hostility they experience as a result.

As Friedan's work created a language and a space to talk about the experience of a generation of unfulfilled American mothers and housewives, I hope that this book too will explode into the public consciousness and lead to a much more nuanced understanding of the experience of so many modern women. We live in an extraordinarily powerful moment to be a woman in the western world – with privileges our deep ancestors could only dream of, and rights that our recent ancestors from the Suffragettes to the second wave feminists of the 1970s fought for. The experience of being childless not by choice, for complex reasons, is one that feminism has dropped the ball on; it is my hope that this book, these testimonies, will begin to redress that balance.

Jody Day
Founder, Gateway Women

---

5   Friedan, B. (1963) *The Feminine Mystique*. London: Victor Gollancz.

Acknowledgements

Thank you to each of the women whose stories are collected here, for their generosity, kindness and courage. Without exception, every one of these women told me that they were motivated to tell their story to help other circumstantially childless women, that those reading their story might judge themselves less harshly, feel less isolated and be more hopeful that a life without a biological child can be one that is rich with love, purpose and challenges, as good lives are.

Thanks to Jody Day for her warm support, and for kindly writing the foreword.

Thanks to Ian Macleod for the breakfasts, the title and the constant love, and to Margaret MacDonald, Liza Wilcox and Richard McLachlan for their encouragement.

Thanks to Emma Hall and Mary Goulter for help in transcribing the long interviews that are the basis of these stories.

And thanks to the team at JKP who recognised the need for these stories to be told publicly, and enabled their publication in such an inclusive and professional way.

Introduction

The first story I heard about circumstantial childlessness was from a woman called Jackie, around 15 years ago. I was a counsellor, working in private practice, specialising in grief issues. Jackie was 36 and single, and she desperately wanted to become a mother. She'd had a series of relationships but none of them had worked out, and she felt like time was running out. 'If it hasn't happened by the time I'm 40,' she said, 'it's all over.'

She talked a lot about the mother she hoped to be, and the children she dreamed of having. She had names for them in her mind, and some little things – tiny clothes and toys, and a book that she had loved as a child – set aside, tucked away for them at home. She told me about her distress when friends or work colleagues announced they were pregnant, and her guilt about not feeling wholehearted in congratulating them. She talked about her shame that she had 'failed' as a woman – in ways she couldn't quite articulate – and her embarrassment and confusion, as a feminist, at feeling that way. She worried that she wouldn't have time to meet someone, for them to get to know one another and start a family, before her fertility ran out.

In the weeks and months after meeting Jackie, I found myself working with many women who were childless by circumstance, women who had expected to conceive and bear a child at some point in their lives and who – as far as they knew – were physically capable of doing so, but for whom it hadn't happened. Their stories were all different, but there were common threads. Women talked about feeling angry and invisible, that there wasn't a place for them in a world designed for parents and families. They struggled with a sometimes overwhelming sadness and sense of loss, but found it hard to pin down what they were grieving for. They felt that in some way their predicament was their fault, because it was the outcome of choices they had made, but looked back and couldn't see where they would have made different decisions. Some felt excitement about the possibilities available to them in a life without children, but worried they'd be blindsided by regret sometime in the future. They resented people's pity, but longed to be better understood. Over and over again they told me how hard they found it to talk to others about their situation, and how isolated, lonely and misunderstood they felt.

The statistics related to how many women remain childless vary from country to country, but circumstantial childlessness does appear to be a growing trend in many places. In Britain, for example, about one in five women is childless,[1] and it is estimated that for 80 per cent of older women childlessness is due to circumstances rather than choice or infertility.[2] A global survey by the Organisation for Economic Co-operation and Development (OECD) estimates that in British women between the ages of 15 and 39, only 0.67 per cent choose to be 'childfree', although elsewhere in the Eurozone that figure rises to 1.5 per cent.[3] And it seems that in that group of British women, only a very few decide from an early age that they do not want to have children; most repeatedly postpone the decision about whether or not to have children until biological constraints make that decision final.[4]

Childlessness is not part of my life story. I am a mother to four children, and a grandmother to four more. But as time went by I heard many more stories, now as a doctoral researcher rather than a counsellor, exploring women's narratives of circumstantial childlessness in order to better

1   Office for National Statistics (2017) Childbearing for women born in different years, England and Wales: 2016 (statistical bulletin). www.ons.gov.uk/peoplepopulationandcommunity/birthsdeathsandmarriages/conceptionandfertilityrates/bulletins/childbearingforwomenbornindifferentyearsenglandandwales/2016

2   Ferguson, D. (2018) 'From older mums to the happily childless: what does Mother's Day mean today?' The Guardian, 11 March, 2018.

3   OECD Family Database (updated 17 December 2016) SF2.2: Ideal and actual number of children. www.oecd.org/els/family/SF_2_2-Ideal-actual-number-children.pdf

4   Berrington, A. (2004) 'Perpetual postponers? Women's, men's and couple's fertility intentions and subsequent fertility behaviour.' Population Trends 117, 9–19.

understand the experience. And it was from that experience of listening to women's stories that the impetus to create this book was born. I became interested in the meanings that having a child and being a mother have for women, and in what was perceived to be lost – or gained – when becoming a parent has not come about. I wondered about other ways women might 'do mothering' in their lives when they have not had a child. I questioned what might be happening in women's social worlds – and more broadly in social structures such as education, the media and the workplace – that they talked about feeling such a strong sense of isolation, misunderstanding and judgment in response to their childlessness. Why was the question 'Do you have children?' so dreaded, and why was it so difficult to talk about to friends, family and work colleagues?

As I read and wrote and listened to women, I found that one of the difficulties of talking about their experience is finding ways to avoid pathologising childlessness. The very word – child*less*ness – defines women in terms of what they are *not*. Some women have consciously chosen to think and speak of themselves as 'childfree', but others told me that while they aspired to 'childfree', they *felt* 'childless'. Socially though, in many parts of the world it is becoming more acceptable for women to choose not to have children. In focusing on women's stories of circumstantial childlessness I am not suggesting that all women *should* have children, are 'meant' to have children, or will be unhappy at some level if they do not become mothers, biological or otherwise. Over and again, these stories illustrate the ways in which women's reproductive decisions are made in the context of extremely complex social messages around mothering, changing social trends related to economic and career trajectories and delayed marriage or partnering.

Weaving through these social factors, and their impact on each woman's life, are the unique threads of her personal life history: her experiences and relationships growing up, and the conscious and unconscious desires and fears about motherhood that are unique to her story. This psychosocial tangle is at the heart of the stories in this book. They illustrate the ways that simple labels like 'childless' and 'childfree' miss the detail of women's life experiences, where ideas about 'choice' – and what it is to be a mother – are much more complex than they first appear.

Some of the women whose stories are told here were part of my original doctoral study. Others contacted me after hearing about the book from Jody Day on the 'Gateway Women' website, from an interview I did on National Radio in New Zealand, or from a post I made on my Facebook page asking for women to contact me if they were interested in telling their story. I talked with women in several different parts of the world, usually face to face in the woman's home or my office, and occasionally by computer or telephone.

As we talked, the story inevitably jumped about – as stories do – and often the telling was interrupted by tears, or perhaps by a cat or dog coming in for some attention. I had questions as starting points, but our conversations roamed in wide-ranging ways. When the recording of each conversation had been transcribed I began the process of editing it, using the woman's words but cutting the story down to a very much shorter one, and rearranging it to make it flow in a linear way while keeping the conversational style.

A story is always shaped in its telling for the audience. I was the audience, and in retelling the story for readers I in turn shaped it again, even though I used the woman's words. My aim was to capture the elements of the story that are important for she who told it, in a way that shows readers something of both the teller and the telling. My guiding principle was that each woman must feel happy about the version of their story that is told here. Many of these stories travelled to and fro across the world several times before we arrived at a version that its teller felt comfortable to be told to a much more public audience. Most women have chosen to use a pseudonym – some because they were protecting others in their story, and others because they preferred to remain unidentifiable themselves – and in some stories women have asked me to distort other potentially identifying features such as their profession or where they live.

Women who are medically infertile will find much in these stories of circumstantial childlessness that overlaps with their experience. In reality, the line between these categories of infertility is blurred, since many women who had no reason to assume that they could not have a child earlier in their lives develop age-related infertility as they grow older. However, the presumption that they *could* have had a child if they had made different choices earlier in their life adds a dimension to the grief many women who tell their stories here feel, and they talk about a painful sense that they are to blame for the predicament they find themselves in.

Circumstantial childlessness is of course not a women-only predicament. Men who would like to become fathers are perhaps the ultimately disenfranchised, since they do not even have the option of having a child on their own. There are many ways in which they too share the experience of women who are childless by circumstance, but their lives are differently socially defined by whether or not they are fathers than women's are by motherhood, and their potential to become a parent is not quite as constrained by the limits of their fertility in terms of time. For these reasons I decided to collect only women's stories for this book, although many of the issues these women raise will resonate for circumstantially childless men as well.

Grief and a sense of loss permeate many of these stories. Unlike most losses, there are no photographs to show or memories to share of something or someone once present, and now gone. What is gone – or at risk of being lost – is the dream of having a child and of becoming a mother, and it is hard to overstate how painful that loss is for many of the women who tell their stories here. For some of these women, the loss is complicated still further by their sense that their childlessness is an outcome of the choices they have made earlier in their lives. Many blame themselves harshly; learning to forgive themselves is a theme that runs though many of these women's stories.

Their stories are not just of sadness though. Women often

spoke of the relief they felt when the possibility of becoming pregnant had passed, and a 'toxic hope' that had held them hostage to the dream of having a child was finally gone. They talked about their awareness that *not* having a child freed up energy, time and resources for extended possibilities that would not be available to them as mothers. Older women talked about a process of adaptation to a life that was different from the one they had expected, but no less valuable or pleasurable. For many this appeared to be a process of mining what motherhood meant to them – the chance to nurture, to be creative or to leave a legacy of some sort – and finding other ways to embody it in their lives.

When I explored circumstantial childlessness as a researcher, many participants in the study talked about the social silence that surrounds their experience. Several explicitly asked me to gather these stories and write this book, to provide a further platform for circumstantially childless women's stories. In reading them, women may be able to make better sense of their own, and other people – professionals, friends, work colleagues and family – might better understand some of the issues that childless women face.[5]

---

5   There are other excellent accounts of circumstantially childless women
     telling their own and one another's stories available, and online and local
     support communities are beginning to grow in many countries. I especially
     recommend the Gateway Women website http://gateway-women.com,
     which offers a number of supports to circumstantially childless women
     including a private online community, notices of events and meetup groups.

But change does not come about unless that silence, and the social norms and expectations that underpin it, are identified and challenged. I have made this collection of personal stories based in my confidence in the capacity of narrative – the power of stories – to illuminate broader social structures and issues and their effects in people's day-to-day lives. Questions about the ways that these structures create the social circumstances which women experience as a personal problem are implicit in these stories. I have been very intentional in gathering and editing them in a way that aims to open up these questions, and to encourage critique. I hope they might contribute to broader public conversations about childlessness, because women's experience will only change when the public stories told about this experience reflect the many-faceted implications it has in women's lives, and the creative and satisfying ways that circumstantially childless women choose to live their lives are validated and valued.

Gina,

43, *Lives in the US*

My mother and her mother both quite consciously raised me as a feminist. They wanted me to feel that I could be anything or anyone, that it wasn't necessary to have a child in order to fulfill myself. My mother said to me several times that the world doesn't need more children, although I think what she was doing was trying to justify her own reluctance to have children, because she was actually my aunt. She's a childless woman, and she raised me – somewhat reluctantly – when her kid sister was killed in the street by a car at the age of 20, and I was two. Her life was turned upside down. I always signalled for her kind of a mixture of terrible grief, joy, burden, reluctance and all kinds of stuff that I don't think I was aware of at that time, but spent most of my teenage years trying to sort through. That's always been a source of my sense of insecurity as a person: feeling kind of like I didn't belong.

When I was 17 I fell in love with a woman, and I realized that there was a whole other world. I leapt suddenly into early

80s gay and lesbian culture in West Coast US. The people I knew talked about marriage as if it was just the tool of the patriarchy, and we didn't talk about having children much at all.

Then things changed again. When I was 22 I got involved with a man, I got pregnant, and I had an abortion. I really kind of flubbed the whole situation pretty badly actually, and – because of the feminist ideology really – I didn't ask him what he thought, so he was iced out, and that was very hard for him. For me there was no question in my mind that I didn't want the child, and I didn't want to be stuck with him. So on one hand it was an easy choice to make because my gut told me that I was right, but afterwards – pretty much immediately – I started feeling that I really would want children in the future. I broke up with that man and I spent the next two years feeling enormous regret about how I had handled the relationship, but it was a really good experience for me I think, because I needed to make a decision about what kind of a person I wanted to be.

I still think about that child. And I feel selfish in a way that I didn't allow myself to feel then, because of the politics of the day: a woman's choice and all that sort of thing. I mean I certainly support the pro-choice movement, but I do see it differently after that experience. I have some regrets; I had the option to terminate that life and I took it. Nobody can ever say whether it was right or wrong that I terminated that pregnancy, but there was a child, and there is a real loss there. There is a *person* there, really, or a potential person. And from time to time I'd think about it, and it's that hopelessness of never knowing what that person would have been like. It's just *hopeless*. So, you tell your brain to just…shut up. There's absolutely no point pursuing it.

By the time I met my husband at 25 I was sure that I wanted children, and I did tell him that. He assumed then that we wouldn't have a relationship, because he already had three, and was sure that he didn't want any more. And that was my dilemma: I was involved with a man who had had a vasectomy, and had a *really* strong sense that he didn't want more children, so it was really my choice. Whenever I looked at it, it was a matter of leaving someone I was in love with for the vague possibility I would find someone else and then produce a child, who I couldn't picture. You know it was all very abstract and it just didn't add up. I had to break it down for my husband one time and say, 'Look, why don't *you* try this out; imagine being in my position. Your calculus is choosing between this abstract scenario that might or might not work out, or this real live person that you're in love with. Don't you *get* that?' And you know, he got it at that point, I think. But there's no discussion socially about what that's *really* like. I mean I'm sure I'm not the only one. Surely not! There's no general recognition that this is a cohort of people.

Very few people talk to me about not having children. I think there is a social attitude that argues that I should have made the decision to leave and, given that I didn't, I don't have any right to gripe about it now. I think the implication is that it's my life, and if I made my choice to stay then I should not feel regret or grief about it. It wipes out any avenue for complaining about it, or even talking about it really. That's a big mechanism at work in women's tendency to stay isolated and not discuss it. As a woman, as soon as you bring something up, you're implicitly seeking emotional support, and you have to have the right to seek that support.

I actually did try to get pregnant one time, by someone else, and that didn't work. It was a desperate and dumb thing to do. I was 35, and at that age you're sort of feeling like, 'This is it; the window's really closing fast!' There were various periods when I'd have long stints surfing the internet looking at IVF and sperm banks, and fostering, and adoption from various countries. But there was something that always stopped me taking that next step. I really wanted to have my *husband's* child. I would have gotten pregnant in an instant if he had wanted to.

I feel kind of resigned and mixed about it now because I think it would have been good. I mean, I agree with my mother that the world doesn't actually need more people in it. I don't feel conflicted about that at *all*. And I've been somebody who has had quite poor health genetically, and I would hate to pass that on. But I think it would have been really wonderful to have had that experience that most women do. I was always very curious about what pregnancy would have felt like – if I'd carried it to term – and to have that experience of really existing for another being, to cut through the selfishness that we all seem to inherit as part of our species. It's a different kind of relationship than you have with people your own age; it's an unconditionality and sense of selflessness. I mean I have a family, and they're wonderful, but I've spent my whole life trying to belong to a family and it always felt like I was just half there. A child would have been a whole one. That's one of the reasons why I really wanted a child I think.

At the time that was really hard. *Really* hard. And sad. I felt sad and as if I didn't belong, and I felt as if I didn't have a signature – that it wouldn't make any difference if I didn't exist.

Maybe I have been able to partially fill that need to belong in other ways though. I don't feel like a terribly unhappy person. And I've talked myself through it. I don't have a friend who has gotten everything they wanted in life; I've never met such a person.

Last year I went to San Francisco for the birth of my godson. I stayed in the family's house for his first two weeks and I was able to hold him every morning while his mother – who is my best friend – took a shower and had a break from him. I'd put my finger in his mouth to stop him crying, and sing to him, and just be there for his first few weeks of life in a way that was *really* precious. It was so cool. She very deliberately gave me that opportunity, I know she did. As far as infancy goes, that is it for me, and it was really special. *Really* special. I felt incredibly fortunate.

I always think about having a child. Every month I think about it. There's a strong element of hope that as I get older I'm not suddenly going to be visited with great regret, and it's all going to get mellower and mellower and that we're all going to be okay, but there is still a nagging worry that I will be blindsided by regret. I'm a grandmother now that my husband's children have had children of their own, and that's great. It's not the same as mothering – and it's better in some ways – but the simple fact of being someone's mother is something I won't ever have.

I don't feel sorry for myself anymore. I don't know if I can take very much credit for that attitude though. I mean when I felt really sorry for myself, I didn't have any control over it. If a woman had a total midlife breakdown about childlessness, I wouldn't begrudge her that at all. That seems really reasonable to me. I just feel…well when you have love in your life, it heals your wounds. My relationship with my husband is really good. *Really* good. It sounds so corny doesn't it, but it's a healing environment that we've created. We've worked really, really hard, and we could have just chucked it in at hundreds of different points. There's a sense of destiny about it now.

So I just feel lucky about everything. Somehow we were lucky enough to excavate love from all of this and live in it. And you know, who knows what will happen in the future?

Toni,

46, Lives in New Zealand

I tried to get pregnant over two periods. The first time I would have been about 27, and I'd been in a long-term relationship with a guy. During the last couple of years of our relationship I started spending more time socialising with women – particularly lesbian women – and I used to joke with him, you know, 'If I ever leave you, it'll be for a woman.' But we loved each other, and we tried for a baby for maybe four or five months. I didn't get pregnant, and then I fell in love with a woman and eventually came out, and that shelved any thought of parenting or trying to become pregnant at that point. A few years later I was in England, staying with a lesbian couple who had children using a donor and self-insemination. And I remember thinking, 'Oh, that's really a possibility and actually it's not that difficult. In fact it's incredibly easy.' It put it back on the agenda for me.

The second time was with my partner Karen. We were in Germany for a year and we decided that would be a great place to try to find a donor. We started networking through lesbian circles and found one quite quickly. He was a straight guy. I remember we were extremely nervous going to meet him, and afterwards I was joking with Karen that he had good teeth. She laughed and said, 'It's like you're looking for a horse!'

We inseminated – oh, maybe four times – before I got pregnant. And I had seven lovely weeks where we were really giddy with excitement. I remember going to bed and just laughing with glee because I'd hit the stage where I'd be ravenously hungry after a big evening meal and couldn't wait for breakfast. We told a few family members, not everyone, but a few people.

And then I miscarried. It was devastating for us both. We tried again as soon as we were allowed, and we tried for the rest of the year, with no luck. When we came back home, we looked for a donor here. We put ourselves on the clinic waiting list, and negotiated with one guy. That didn't pan out, and it was very frustrating because after initially committing, he wouldn't follow through. After he didn't respond to several suggestions for setting up a meeting together to talk over details, we realised that he must have changed his mind and didn't know how to tell us. So we stopped leaving him messages and never heard from him again.

It was a really hard time, and not so long after that, Karen decided she didn't want us to continue trying. I think the grief about the miscarriage, and all the difficulties with trying to find a donor after it; for her it just became too hard.

It was a really big thing for me, because I felt like I had

to make a decision about what that meant for me, and our relationship. I never felt the relationship was at risk, but I suppose that romantic ideal of us seeing ourselves as two mums, as opposed to her being my partner who was supportive of me being a mum; it just felt different. And so...I hummed and haahed for a long time, and over time the grief just lessened and I just slowly let go of it. It's the incremental process of letting go.

Throughout much of this time I was part-time parenting my niece Emily, who's now 21. In fact, she lived with me for half of each week from the time she was 18 months old right up until she left home just a few years ago. I've always felt that I would still like to have a biological child myself – and experience pregnancy and give birth and all of that – but having her in my life helped soften that longing, because I was a part-time parent/auntie.

Emily's relationship with her Mum now is different to her relationship with me. I'm the backup if her Mum's out of cell phone range or on holiday, and sometimes I feel a bit envious of that relationship. I'd like to be the first port of call! But her relationship with me is also quite different to the relationship with her other two aunts; they're ordinary aunts, and she doesn't ring them up crying when things are going badly in her life. So it's not the same as being her mum, but it's more than just being an aunt. And having her all these years has still given me a relationship of watching a child grow: being involved in decisions about her wellbeing and her daily life, making her school lunch, picking her up from school, supervising homework.

All my life in that role though I've suffered from lack of recognition of the part I play in her life, and that's hurt. It really hurts; it still hurts now. I think there are times where I've had to try to protect myself a bit from those feelings. I remember at Emily's 21st there was a family friend there who knows and continues – it seems to me – to forget the role I have had in Emily's life. She saw a photo of Emily on her first day at school with her Mum. We were all sitting outside our place and she said, 'Oh that's nice, she popped in to show off her school outfit.' And I just thought, 'No, actually her mother had popped in, to wish her well on her first day at school. Emily was with me and I was taking her off to school.' Her Mum was quite good at recognising what I did, but other people often didn't seem to have a framework for managing that.

So now? You know, I look at pregnant women and I just think they look incredibly beautiful. And to see that expanding belly…I think it just must be such an exciting time. I mean, that's also romanticised. I've had friends who've had horrific pregnancies where they've been sick every single day. But still, I love the idea of seeing my growing belly, and nourishing the baby, and experiencing childbirth and breastfeeding. Yeah, I really, really, really warmed up to that. I still think it would be lovely.

Overall, there's been a quiet sense of loss but I've accommodated it into my life. And in a way, I don't see it as a bad thing. I can almost treasure that loss of what could have been. Occasionally we talk about how old that baby would have been, if it had been meant to be. And my mother

– wildly excited in the first seven weeks of that pregnancy – had managed to whip up a pair of booties and sent them to us in Germany, and I've kept those as a wee memento. Very occasionally I'll have a little look at those.

So it's kind of bittersweet. Sweet that we had that little brief taste, those short weeks of dreaming about that life. And sorrow and sadness that it didn't eventuate. I don't really think I've got deeper grief buried that I haven't dealt with, but I do occasionally wonder whether that will change. I haven't gone through menopause yet, and I wonder whether that might be a period when I think 'Oh well I've really done it now.' Or when I'm 80, whether I might experience a different grief then. I don't know.

I'll have to wait and see.

Andrea,

47, *Lives in England*

There are so many bits to explain; it's quite tricky to unpick it all.

My Mum always used to say there's no point in having regrets; you've got to deal with where you are now. And that sustains me – the regret doesn't eat me up – but I wish... maybe if I'd had some kind of therapy sooner, if someone had seen that I was struggling, that I still had a lot of issues from my parents' divorce. I wish my Mum had said, 'You really need to think about this.' But you start your career, reach your targets, you progress, you go through the hoops, and then you step up to the next level...and that was the way life was. I mean, there were millions of points where things could have been different, but understanding what happened to me at nine explains so much of that. If that hadn't have happened, I wonder if my life would have turned out very differently.

What happened is that my parents divorced. My Dad had an affair and left my Mum to start a new family. At the time,

I was utterly devastated. I don't know how to describe it. I think part of the legacy of my parents' divorce was that I felt that marriage or having children wasn't for me; that was for *other* people. And that's the thing I really regret: the limits of what I interpreted then as possible for me. There's not enough understanding of the effects of divorce on children I think, and I wonder if that's an issue for other women, and why they haven't had children.

I went to university and did further study, and then got a job in publishing, and I was very, very focused on that. I wouldn't say I rose quickly, but I went up the ladder at a pace and that was all-consuming. I met my partner David quite late on, at around 40.

Around the time we got together my Mum became ill and died, and in a way that solidified things for me about what I hadn't done in my life and what I wanted to do. I thought a lot about passing things on, about generations and how they're replicated, and what losing my mother meant. Being a mother for me is definitely something around legacy, not just material goods, but what you pass on as a way of being. The idea of carrying on my mother's line and her genes somehow felt very important around that time: her continuing in the world in some way.

David and I tried for a bit to get pregnant naturally. Someone in an IVF clinic said, 'Oh I think you'll be fine naturally,' and I rue her for saying that because it put us back a few years. When I'd just turned 42 we went to an IVF clinic, and it all worked perfectly! I couldn't believe it! I'd got in under the wire I thought; I was pregnant first time.

Everything went fantastically for a while. I was so impressed with myself. We got through the 12-week mark – I would expect some kind of tragedy to have occurred every time I'd go to the bathroom – and we'd had all those tests for anomalies, and got through that too. I was kind of relaxing into it, and then at the 20-week scan things went tragically and awfully wrong. There was a problem with the placenta and it wasn't letting the baby grow. They said it was 50/50 which way it could go, and we had six weeks of not knowing whether she would be okay or not. They were aiming for the point where they could take her out and support her outside the womb.

I took time off work and I just ate and ate as much as I could, and tried not to move. That was my theory that seemed like it might help, because the doctors had no advice at all about what would help. I would have done absolutely anything they suggested, but there just isn't enough research done into the condition to know what will help. I wanted to break down and cry, but I thought I shouldn't because that might upset the baby, so I tried to stay calm and relaxed.

At 27 weeks, her heart stopped.

Stillbirth is very hard to deal with; it just rips all sense of hope from you. I'd heard of it of course, but it happens to other people, doesn't it? It doesn't happen to you. I used to think of it as other people having a colour photo version of childbirth, and I had the black and white negative version. It was the lowest low I've ever been; I didn't feel suicidal, but I didn't want to live.

After our daughter died I was just totally focused on how to get pregnant again. That was the only thing that I thought about every day. I did so much reading and research into it, and I had a plan. For me it's not about replacing her but…maybe it's about having got to the halfway mark with being pregnant: having been in that maternal world and having a glimpse of it. Since then we've done one round of IVF with my own eggs, two rounds with donor eggs, and we're gearing up for our third go soon, also with donor eggs.

I feel as if I'm perpetually stuck in a cycle of trying to have a child with IVF. Your whole life is on hold. But I think if we ever got to the point where we decided we weren't going to try anymore, life just seems like an open savannah of desert. What do we do then? Do we just sit around until we die?

One of my old school friends is visiting from abroad in a few months, and we're having a big meetup together with other people I went to school with. I imagined we'd all go out for dinner, but then I had this slow realisation that it will be an in-the-day event. People will have their children there, and they will all be talking about them. My daughter – and my motherhood – is invisible to them. It's a strange no-man's land: this liminal feeling of being a mother, and yet not a mother. I feel as if I tried to be a mother and failed at it. The fact that I won't be recognised as a mother, or that she wouldn't be talked about, means that I am panicking about how I can get out of this event. Can I go on holiday? Can we just leave the country when it's happening?

There's another part of all of this that I find it hard to make sense of too. I'm thinking about the messages that women are told and that I was told growing up. I mean, when

I was growing up in about the 1980s and 1990s I just wouldn't have been friends with anyone if their ambition was to be a stay-at-home mum. That seemed the most banal thing you could do with your life to me. You had to be a strong woman who wanted a career and prove that you could survive on your own without a man. But for some reason I seemed to take that message in a very either/or, black and white way, in a way my friends and peers didn't. I think suffering from a lack of self-esteem hasn't helped me, and the career ladder was the easier option for me, compared with the messiness of relationships and family life.

So now, *of course* I believe women should have jobs and equality, but I also realise the loveliness of that kind of life that somehow felt very closed off for me. I've absolutely loved my job, and I've worked way too hard and long days.

But I just think that's not the only way to live now.

Lynne,

39, Lives in New Zealand

I was an in-the-moment kind of kid. I didn't dwell on whether I'd have children, but I always thought I would, in the way that girls did back then. I had a fairly conventional family upbringing – Mum and Dad and three kids in the suburbs kind of thing. I didn't think about a career; I'd need a *job* for a while but I didn't think I'd need a career, because I'd do what Mum did, and be at home with the kids.

When the time came to have children, I had ended up in a relationship with a man who already had a child, and very definitely didn't want more. I let that relationship drag on for far too long, from about 25 to 37 or so. Once I hit my mid-30s, I was trying to pull away, with us both acknowledging that if I wanted to have children I needed to find another relationship, but I found it hard to get away from him, and when I did try, he was quite possessive and wanted me back.

During that time I looked into having children as a solo mum. I got as serious as contacting a gay guy who was also looking to have a child and said he was interested in a co-parenting arrangement, where we would have shared the child's care. But it ended up that he had already had a child and was himself in a really messy relationship, which just freaked me out.

Around that time I had a bad bout of depression, and by 37, 38, I started to feel much more ambivalent about having children. I felt a lot older somehow. I was having a few minor health issues, and I was feeling like it would be hard to have a child. I found myself starting to look at what else I could do with my life that would be fulfilling. So when I met my husband – and I knew from the outset that he couldn't have children, and didn't want them as well – I was open to that relationship.

It's a fantastic relationship, and I feel blessed. It's ironic really – given how much I wanted to have a child – that the last couple of years have been the happiest of my life... without children!

Now that I've realized I'm not going to have children I do feel some grief around it because...if I really try to feel not having a child I am left with quite deep feelings of having missed the opportunity to nurture. I wanted to have the experience of being a mother, and of pregnancy. I don't think I'm unrealistic about how hard it is, or can be – especially on your own – but I think of it as living life to the full, in a way.

And I still would like the experience of a baby growing in my body, and suckling on my nipple. I think of it as a loss, and...I *feel* it, quite physically. For me, it's stuff that I find hard to explore, or articulate. I'd like to understand it better and put it aside, put it away, but I don't know how to do that.

It comes up quite often, like when I'm with my husband's family; there are no children in the family and I feel an absence there. I like people, and I like big families. I liked the idea of creating my own family. I enjoy having the diversity of having lots of different people around and there's a sense of loss there, of not building that for myself. And not seeing my husband reflected in another person. I'm still...you know I love him deeply and I love the idea – the sort of fascination – of seeing him, or parts of him, in another person. I do find that kind of cool. I suppose I'm wanting to have a little...him, in a way.

One of the reasons I use the word grief when I think about not having a child might also be because I've actually had two abortions. The second one particularly I found very difficult. I was really ambivalent about it; I actually wanted to have children, but the guy who was the father didn't and...I just felt this enormous pressure not to have it. I know it might sound really weak, to have given into that, but he was incredibly dominating. You have compulsory counselling as part of the process, and what made the whole experience most difficult was that I had gone into that wanting to talk about it. The woman I saw was just so angry with me – that I would choose that option, particularly in my mid-30s – and I came out of the session with her a heaving mess. It was one of the most traumatic times I've ever had. I hated her so much that I couldn't actually respond to her; I think I said about three words in total.

To be honest though I think I would probably make the same decision now. I can't say that I haven't had choices because obviously I have, and I've…sort of made them. But I guess with the two abortions I didn't feel like I had a whole lot of choice really. I mean, theoretically I did, but the thing is you don't just make choices for yourself, do you? That was the thing with my husband and previously – with the father of that child – I was very aware of what their choices would be as well. I have quite a strong sense of responsibility for not making choices that aren't right for other people as well. I know one woman who pretty much tricked a man into getting her pregnant, and she wasn't worried about his choice of not wanting a child at all. I think women do use that power of being able to get pregnant, as much as they have the burden of it as well.

So I have a sense of loss there, and even just talking about it now I can feel the emotion in my body. The abortions made me realize how hard decisions are, and how messy life is sometimes.

They made it really difficult for me to talk to people about my feelings about not having had a child – the irony of wanting children and having had two abortions. I mean, they're contradictory feelings, and unless you know the detail about what happened, it wouldn't make sense to most people. There just aren't many opportunities to talk it through. And bringing up abortion – boy! For me…it goes really deep. There are times when I really could have done with some support, and I know I can't be the only woman who has gone through some of the thoughts and angst that I've been through. A good counsellor would have been good, but you just don't know what you're getting.

There are other, smaller losses too. I've missed out on some of the camaraderie that there is between my colleagues at work who do have children. There's lots of comparing notes about schools and all that sort of stuff. It's the topic of conversation at morning tea. I just switch off to it really. I mean I'm vaguely interested in their kids too, because they're nice kids. But there's a big part of that stuff that I don't take part in.

I think some women have been curious about why I haven't got children, and there are assumptions about how much freedom that gives me. I get snide comments that I don't have to worry about all the things that they have to worry about because they've got children. I think it's about as close as both men and women get to admitting that it's quite hard having children and if they had the choice again they wouldn't necessarily make it. A moment of ambivalence maybe.

I feel a sense of freedom in some ways; not having children has given me a bit more focus about what I do with the rest of my life, in my career and pursuing some of my interests, and taking a bigger role as an auntie to my sister's children. I'd like to consolidate a career a bit more in the future, and I have more energy for it now. I've always been interested in government – I was quite a political activist in my 20s – and maybe eventually I'll go back to that. I just want to contribute somehow – I guess we all do – to making the world a better place.

It's some relief to me that by not having children I am having a much smaller footprint on the world, and for my husband, that's the biggest reason. So there's that, and the other thing is that my husband and I are quite keen to set ourselves up with a more sustainable kind of life: a bigger veggie garden, we've got bees, we want to get chickens, that kind of thing.

I think the future will be fine. We've got enough in our lives, and in our dreams, that we will have fulfilling lives. I'm pretty confident about that.

Molly,

44, Lives in New Zealand

Sometimes I put my finger on my pulse point. I remind myself that even though I got turned down to adopt a child, and even if I feel useless and I don't matter, I am still alive. There is still a point to me and I've still got something useful to do in the world. And I've got to make the most of it even though there are days when it's very difficult.

I'm still alive.

When I was around 38, I met a guy through a mutual friend, and it got serious quite quickly. He had adult children and he told me he'd love to have more children but he'd had a vasectomy and he'd get it reversed. So I dropped out of the adoptive process, although I was thinking that we'd have that there in the background if things didn't work out. When we went back to the clinic the doctor told us we'd need to have IVF to have a child. Then they checked me and found that I have quite a few gynaecological problems, and I'd need a more invasive procedure than regular IVF. I got quite upset by this so I said to my partner, 'Well look, I've always wanted to adopt so why don't we do that instead,' and he said, 'Yes, okay,' and we started looking into it. We had to live together for three years before we could apply, so we moved in together and everything was going fine. And then, abruptly, my partner changed his mind about adopting.

So we broke up. I didn't really stop to think about it; I had already been upset about the fact that we couldn't have children together. But I still was really keen on adopting, so I moved out, waited for a year and then reapplied to adopt. I was coming up to 42.

I was accepted for the initial stages of the adoption process. That all took over a year, and eventually I got to the second part of the process where you are given a social worker and they come and interview you at your home several times over several months. In my second meeting they started getting concerned about my levels of anxiety, but I have to say anybody going through the adoption process – especially if they've also experienced infertility – is going to be very anxious because a lot is riding on it. So yes, I was really anxious and I don't think there's anything wrong with that.

Anyway, I was called in for a meeting with the boss of the agency, my social worker and her manager, and they said, 'You've got two choices. We can stop the process now or you can ask us to provide a report based on what we know so far, and this will go to a review panel, and they'll make a decision.' I said I would like to take the second option. In the report the social worker made some upsetting comments about my upbringing.

Normally when a prospective adopter's report is written it gets sent to the individual or couple so they can make changes, but I didn't get that opportunity. A lot of the things they wrote in it were wrong; they made assumptions and I never had a chance to refute them. Then the panel turned me down.

My appeal went to a different panel and they said I should be allowed to continue to adopt, but my social workers argued that they didn't have all the information, and therefore they wouldn't accept their decision. In October that year – a year after the whole thing began – they told me they wouldn't take it any further, and I had to withdraw my application. I was devastated. But I just had to accept that my journey to adopt had ended.

I blamed myself. I felt very ashamed because I felt like I was publicly told I wasn't good enough to be a parent. I used to walk around feeling like I had something on my forehead that said 'Unfit Mother' and everybody would see it. And – except for one person – everybody from the adoption group I was in dropped me like a hot potato, because they thought I would be a risk to their adoption process.

Being a mother would have been an opportunity for me to give an adopted child a good start in life; to love them and cherish them, and nurture them, and support them in their wishes and dreams. To pass things on to another generation: my own passions and love for things like theatre and reading. I would have offered a good home to a child. I would have worked hard to give them opportunities. If they wanted to do football – even though I can't bear sport and if they didn't want to do drama, which is one of my passions – I would have totally stood on a wet and muddy football pitch, shouting my head off. I would have done it to let them achieve what they wanted to achieve, to encourage them to be what they wanted to be and have a bit of fun. I would have been a good mother. I would have got things wrong and I would have messed up but I would have got things right too. And I would have been part of a community of other women; whether it's through adoption or birth it doesn't matter how you got the child, you're a mum.

The worst time was when they told me they were stopping the process. Since then it's got easier, but there's lots of little pinpricks every day. Like today, when I went out to a school to see some of the kids I support as part of my work. The mums were all there dropping their kids off, hugging them and everything, and that made me feel really sad. I will never do that; I will never have that experience, never be hugged by my own child, never see them play. It's all that kind of stuff and that happens several times a day. I will always wish that things had turned out differently but they didn't, and there's absolutely nothing I can do about it. I do know I tried as hard as I could. I don't think anybody could have tried harder than me, to make it work.

I was watching *The Wizard of Oz* the other day. I love it when Dorothy sings 'Somewhere over the Rainbow'; it's one of my favourite songs. And when she was singing 'there's a place where your dreams come true' I found myself thinking that over the rainbow and this side of the rainbow are two places: over the rainbow is where I would have had children, and this side of the rainbow I don't. Actually though, one side isn't better than the other. They're just different.

It had a really big impact on me. It made me think that, yes my dream hasn't come true – that dream – but other dreams may. I'm still alive, and I have to start living.

Leeann,

42, Lives in Australia

I sometimes quip to people that 'I forgot!' when they ask why I didn't become a mother, particularly to people that I don't really want to discuss it with. Maybe I'm too much of a psychologist at heart, but I often wonder how consciously or unconsciously we choose things. There's a whole heap of things that sit underneath our 'choices' – our reasons for allowing a situation to develop – that I'm interested in. Because of course you don't 'forget'; you're always conscious, you're always aware that time is ticking. There are enough environmental cues around and well-meaning friends that ask, so how consciously or unconsciously do you make that choice?

Having children was one of those things that was just at the back of my mind as an organic process that of course would happen, one day. Never a plan, but not a plan not to, either. It would come along in its own sweet time. I didn't really have a fairytale view that I would have X amount of children by Y date.

On the face of it, it was a combination of things that stopped that happening, in my case: my decision to pursue a career, a partner who was not particularly interested in children, and a circle of friends who didn't have a lot of children either. So, it just wasn't something that was in my face, if I could put it that way.

At 38 I broke up with my partner, after a 14-and-a-half-year relationship. And it was actually around that time that I went, 'Well if I'm going to have children this would be the time to pursue that, either with a new partner or on my own.' It was my 'If not now, when?' moment. And it just didn't happen. At the time my decision was a little bit more pragmatic than anything else. 'This is going to cost money. It's going to take time and effort. Do I really want it that badly?'

But it's both a logical and an emotional decision to some extent. And certainly, even with my friends' children, I'd always had moments; you know where you're with an adorable child being an absolute angel, and you just think, 'Oh, I can have one of those!' And then, of course, the next second they're not adorable. So I never felt strongly enough, I guess, that this would be something I would need to push for. There was an interest in having children, and an expectation in some ways that I would, but not an overwhelming urge like some people seem to suggest that they have. And not something that pushed through my comfort zones at any particular age or stage. It wasn't an especially difficult decision; it was difficult in an emotional sense, but not in a decision-making sense. It was fairly easy to make on the basis that honestly, if you don't consistently want to do it…then you shouldn't do it. It's kind of like having a tattoo: if you can't decide on the same design for more than a week at a time you probably shouldn't get one.

But underneath all that were the less conscious reasons and they meant a different set of questions to ask myself. I realized I still think of myself as quite young. My gynaecologist would tell you a very different story, in terms of my biological age, but I guess I just never kind of thought I was ready. And it was that fear that I wasn't ready that was at the heart of putting it off. I think that was the period of time, after my partner had left – good timing! – and I had gone through a restructure, my job had been made redundant, and I'd had a heart attack, that I realised I had to make an adult decision about what I was going to do. I had that moment of deciding the pros and cons of which way I went: 'What am I actually afraid of? What might happen; the good things that might happen, but also what are the bad things that might happen?' There was a fear of failure that I recognize from other parts of my life – 'What if I'm not good at this?' I tried to put myself in the shoes of someone who has failed at being a mother, you know – what would that feel like? Because I'm going to be on my own. 'What if I get a child who doesn't sleep through the night? How much resilience do I really have – after going through all these other things – and what mechanisms would I call upon within myself and without myself to be able to deal with those? What if I feel like I've failed?', even if there was nothing objective to suggest that I had. And that's the hard one to get to grips with, because you don't know whether you will fail – or spectacularly succeed – until you do.

And after all of that, I couldn't hand on heart say that I felt consistently enough about wanting to have a child to overcome the weight of all of those logical and emotional reasons for being a little bit hesitant.

So that decision was fairly easy, but coming to realize that there were implications for that non-decision – which had become a decision – was harder. It was the emotional stuff around 'Am I the sort of person who's not going to have children then? If so, what does that mean?' 'Why do other people have children?', you know, 'Is that still something – despite me having decided that it's too expensive, and too much effort – is it still something that I need? Can I get the feelings of parenthood somewhere else?' Those were the questions.

A lot of it was about identity really. I had already had this thought, not only just about whether I would have my own children, but also whether I would be a carer of others. I have a couple of friends who are long-term carers of children, through the State. 'Can I imagine having a child' – as in a foster child – 'or can I imagine having a baby, and what would that look like in my life?' But also, 'What would it offer to the child?' And I think that one of the things that really helped me to become okay with the decision was that I have a number of people in my life who have children, and I am absolutely part of their children's lives. Even in the last four years I'm starting to reap the benefits of that in them coming to me with problems that they're not prepared – or able or wanting – to take to their parents. I didn't see that special auntie role in someone else's life as something I was giving up. It's about finding other ways to make sure that that need within me is met and you don't feel it as a void. It's not a void; I still mother my friends! I certainly mother their children.

What I was giving up is my own kind of mum-ship, if that's a word. And also my kinship, then, with other mums. As you grow older you inevitably lose touch with friends whose paths diverge from yours, and that was becoming evident around that 35 age for me. So at that time of deciding not to pursue having children it was also about making a conscious decision to retain my friendship with these women who were becoming mums and saying, 'Bring your daughter. We're not going to have more than a quick cup of tea, and that's okay.' It was that strategy, I guess, to keep my friendships that also allowed me to remain part of that group, because I had been part of the child-rearing process for a lot of those friends of mine. I wasn't a mum, but I was a mum by default. I'm still friends with a number of people that I've known since pre-school, and that's a long time to give up. So I'm not giving it up. I don't care if it involves baby dribble. It's okay.

But emotionally there is still a 'what if?' scenario that – despite the best of the logical brain – sometimes comes up. There's a residual wondering what I would have been like as a mother. I wonder where it would have taken me. I wonder what I would have learned. I wonder what we, the family unit of any kind that we created, would have been like. I wonder what my child would have gone on to do. I think I missed contributing to the potential for this human being to go on and do good things. I'm sure every mother hopes that their children do good things; some of them, statistically, don't obviously. But it's that wondering, you know – if you're going to be totally egotistical – what breakthroughs of science would my child have created? How proud could I have been if they were, you know, a famous writer or a politician that actually did something? They're the potential, I guess, for the future. And, yeah, I guess I won't know.

So it is creating a form of legacy, and also the opportunity for that to be both ways. You know, I think back to my relationship with my own parents and for everything I learnt, they also learnt. And for everything they've taught me, they learnt as well. It's a great potential for both you and your child, and I think if anything, that's the loss I feel. How enriched would I have felt to be a mother? How much more capacity to love might I have experienced? I mean you experience those things in every relationship that you're in, but to me it just seemed that motherhood is a…I don't know whether it is a *special* relationship, but certainly a very different relationship to any other. And that relationship experience, you know, you can proxy it as much as you like but it's not real until you have to deal with the 3am meltdowns on your own. So, yeah. It's a different kind of feeling.

I see pregnancy as a potential until it actually happens. It's nice to have that potential, even if it's not realized. I don't know how I'll be when the menopause hits and I don't have it.

I must admit, I was away camping in January and I was getting all hot flushy and I was like, 'Oh, I've started! Oh my gosh!' and then I found out that I actually had Ross River Fever! It gave me a little tiny chance to go, 'how do I feel about that? Is that okay?' Not that I really had a great deal of time to reflect on it, but I found my response was more, 'Oh this is going to be annoying,' and that was about it.

I will never know where having children would have taken me. I chose not to do that; I chose to take a decision in the opposite direction, and I still don't know where that's going to take me either. But you've got to at some point stop thinking about it, and just go, well, the decision has been made. And go on with it, either way. The fact that you have children or don't have children, the fact that they talk to you or don't talk to you, the fact that they've done well or not; that's all in the lap of the gods to some extent. You can't think too much about that, you'll drive yourself crazy. There's not enough red wine to deal with that!

Bron,

38, Lives in New Zealand

Around 30, I felt like my life was ready for having children. I was single for most of my 20s, and it never really occurred to me to be thinking about children then. When I saw friends with their children I'd always got a bit of a pang thinking 'I'd love that one day', but it was always 'one day, one day'. I didn't have any burning desires to do something else left. I'd come back home from travelling and working overseas, got a kitten – as you do – and was starting to look for a house, and it was then that I thought, 'Yeah, I could do that.'

But my 30s started passing without me meeting anyone. When I was about 34 a girl I knew decided to ask someone she knew to father a child for her. I was stunned! And a friend's Mum said to me, 'That's what you should do, Bron. You know there's plenty of guys out there. Or go to a pub one night and pick someone up.' I was just like, 'You've got to be joking!' Why set yourself up to deliberately be a single mother, for your children to deliberately not have a father? That to me was incredibly selfish and there was no way I was going to think along those lines. I could see why others would do it but it's not the reason why you have a child. For me it's more about loving someone and caring about them enough that you'd want to create a being that joins you together.

Now I'm 38, and I'm only now in a relationship where I can see myself actually wanting to have children with the guy I'm with. But he's got two children from his previous relationship and he had never thought about having more. He worries that having a child with me would take something away from the two boys that he has now. And I'm 38, he's 42 so he's thinking, by the time they get off your hands you're retired and that's it. We're in a situation where financially it's possible; we could do it if we wanted to, we'd just downsize or whatever. So the door's not completely closed, but it's probably about 99 per cent closed. We probably won't have one.

When I see people pregnant, and they're rubbing their belly, my heart goes because I think, 'Wouldn't it feel wonderful having something growing inside you, and knowing that you are growing it?' But then, with the idea of the actual birth itself I think, 'Oh well, at least I'm not having to go through *that* side of things. And I've got enough stretch marks without being pregnant!' When I was in my 20s there weren't very many people I knew having babies, but now I'm in my 30s I hear more of those stories and part of me thinks, 'Oh, thank goodness.' But then I'll hear a good story and I'll think, 'Oh, I'd love that.' You know?

My partner's two boys are only just four and six now, and

I've been with him for two years, so I feel like I get enjoyment out of them, and I can use my nurturing instincts. We don't see them enough, and we're trying for shared custody but there are a lot of issues as far as their mother is concerned. She keeps trying to tell them that it's, you know, Mum, Dad and the two boys – that's their family. One of them last night – the six–year-old – said, 'You're not part of our family, Bron,' and it wasn't malicious or anything, it was just a statement. I said, 'Well you know, you make up your own mind about who's part of your family but I feel like you're part of my family.' I don't take 'family' from a biological point of view – from a blood point of view – I take it from how you feel and where you feel safe and those sorts of things. He's made a few comments along those lines and it hurts, but I just think to myself that's just come from his Mum so I won't panic too much about it. I have to remind myself that he is a sensitive six-year-old, still finding his way about everything.

Mother's Day was hard last year. I didn't want a Mother's Day present but I wouldn't have minded some sort of acknowledgement about the roles that I do play in the boys' lives. I'm caring for them like a mother when they're with us but, apart from by my partner, that's not recognized by others as being a valid mother: you know, where you nurture them and care for them, and they abide by your rules, and we make sure they have guidelines and all those sorts of things. But then when we're round at their mother's place it's like I have to put a zipper on my mouth because I'm not allowed to say anything.

It's basically only in my own home that I can be a mother to them, but anywhere else, it's taken away from me. I know that that's going to be an aspect of our lives for the next 15 or so years; that I won't have any rights. It feels like mothering to me, but I guess I just play a support role.

I used to think, 'How come other people get to be a mum? Why hasn't that happened for me?' Now it's more being thankful for what I do have. But it could change overnight if he was to wake up tomorrow morning and say that he wanted a child. Because we've thought about it; we have discussed it openly, a number of times. And I see him every now and then looking at a cute wee girl and I think he's thinking, 'I wonder what a girl would be like?'

If he said he'd changed his mind, I think I'd feel all of the emotions. I'd have all of them. Obviously I'd be quite elated, but I'd also be very scared and apprehensive. Probably even feel a little bit confused? Like, is this really the right thing to do? I guess the elation would come from those feelings that I've been…suppressing or putting to aside. The feelings like, 'Wow, yeah, I would actually get to be a mum!' Yeah. I haven't doused that flame entirely. I would still have those feelings.

I am reasonably practical in the sense that if you dwell on something or if you wish for something that is not going to happen you end up digging yourself into a big hole of depression and it's just not worth it. It's not worth putting that sort of pressure on myself. First and foremost, it's him I want in my life. I'd much rather have him in my life and no children, rather than him not in my life and have a child to goodness knows who. I may never lose that feeling that it's not quite the same as having your own. It does pull at my heartstrings, it certainly does, that I can't be called someone's mum.

But we're not all meant to be mums.

Persephone,

44, Lives in England

Whenever I've been having moments of going, 'Oh, fuck, what am I doing?' I have this sudden picture of a little boy or a little girl turning around to me and saying, 'Mummy'. And it makes me smile. I'll be on the bus, thinking, 'Oh God! Oh God', and that picture will pop into my head and I'll be smiling out loud. Being a mother is love, isn't it? Just love. Protection. Being on a journey. Being on a brand new journey.

I always thought that I would be with someone and I would have a family. But it was almost like an imaginary idea, and actually I don't know what I truly ever believed would happen. Like, now I'm imagining having a pregnant tummy, and stroking it, and I know in my mind what it looks like, but I don't think I ever did that before. I think I've been deeply frightened of being in a committed relationship, because of what happened in my childhood and the difficulties and hardships. You know, Mum would get a gas bill and she'd go to bed for three days. Back in the 1970s I was branded a single parent child, and I remember all that lack. It was horrible, and it kind of defined who I was. I didn't want to do that.

I fell pregnant when I was with my second proper boyfriend. I was 27, I wasn't earning very much money, and I just couldn't really see a way of it happening. He…it was the whole 'I'll do whatever you want to do but I don't want this' business. I just thought I couldn't tie myself to someone, and I didn't have the balls to do it on my own. Me, him and my Mum went to a clinic to have the termination. And that was that. I do think about it. The child would have been 16 – God, that's bloody crazy – and my life would have been so different. But I know that I did the right thing.

I was around 35 when I met my last serious partner. I'd joined a dating website and I'd had a couple of dating disasters, and he was my mate that I would go 'Oh my God!' to about them. We became friends, and then we both just went, 'Let's do this.' So I rented my flat out, and moved in with him. We were saving, we were going to get a house and we were going to have children. I had my own video production company at this point, and I was kind of fed up because I wasn't making any money really. But I got offered a new job which was a huge step up for me – basically running a much bigger production company and looking after nine directors – and I remember him saying to me, 'So, what's this going to mean for our baby plans?' And I went, 'Well, you know, I can't take that job and then leave because I'm pregnant, we're going to have to put that on hold,' kind of thing. I felt like I had all the time in the world. I did, I thought I had all the time in the world. I just felt really young and I didn't feel ready, to be honest. Actually, you know, 35, 36, is kind of pushing it a bit, but I'm in an industry where we're all in this forced sense of youth.

I don't think he was very happy about it, and we split up, a week after my 37th birthday. And that was a bit like, 'Oh, fuck'. Also, because it was my 37th birthday, I think maybe that was the beginning of me going, 'I can see 40.' Basically though, it was the best thing that happened, because that was when I revisited my spiritual beliefs, and suddenly I was like, 'Who am I? What do I like?' I started rowing – because I'd always wanted to row – I did meditation and I took up kundalini yoga. And I got serious about having a child. I still thought I had plenty of time. Then three or four months ago I went to a clinic to check my fertility status and I was thinking, 'Well, I'll get told I've got four or five years. They'll probably ring me up and tell me I'm the most fertile 43-year-old they've ever come across on the planet, and that still gives me a few years to meet someone.'

Instead they told me I was in perimenopause. I didn't take it in properly at the beginning; I was just like, '*What*?' I didn't know what questions to ask. I was not expecting it. It was a huge shock. Huge shock. Maybe it is just my peers, and my industry, but there is this thing that we can kind of have it all. You know, I've been drinking and smoking my face off for the last 25 years; it's almost stupid that I thought that there was going to be no effect on my body. Since I got the news I've grieved a bit for my body really, because I feel like in a way that I've cheated it. I've not allowed it to experience something that it was meant to experience.

You know, I don't think fertility is on many people's radar before they try to get pregnant. I think everyone just thinks, 'It's going to happen! It's going to happen! It's going to happen! Oh fuck, it's not going to happen.' In fact, most of my friends who are in relationships are doing one form or other of IVF. And I know that I've sat and had conversations with people and I go, 'Don't worry about it, it *is* going to happen,' and in the back of my head I'm thinking, 'Well that's not going to happen to me; it's going to be fine for me.' I just think I'm going to meet someone and I'm going to make a fabulous baby. Four or five years ago one of my friends suggested that I freeze my eggs, but even then I just felt like to freeze my eggs would be saying that it's not going to happen. I was so stuck in the belief that the right person was going to come into my life. Blind belief. It's so Disney it's kind of stupid. You know, I believe in manifestation and magnetising into my life and I think that was probably why it's been such a shock. It's been like, 'Oh shit, the belief in my belief has let me down! Oh my God, I've trapped myself into this.' Sort of being asleep.

So now I'm doing fertility treatment. What I don't want is to wake up at 50 – which is, what, six years away – and to look back at this time in my life and go, 'Why didn't I try?' I have to try, I think. I'm basically saying that I'm going to try this once, but really, I think I'll probably give it two goes. And if it doesn't work, then that's…enough's enough. I will already be setting up a more holistic, more spiritual, slower paced life – because I just don't want to keep up with the lifestyle that I'm leading – and then the world's my oyster, isn't it? I can maybe find somebody who's got children, or I could go back to my original plan and look into adoption.

I do imagine the child. If I have a girl she will be called Dulce Aurelia Florence. And if I have a boy, it will be Devon Elliot Axel. I've had these names since I decided that I was going to do this, and I always thought I would have a boy first. I never kind of really visualised them before, and now, because of what I'm going to be doing, I'm like, I'm almost being God, because I'm creating a baby using donor sperm and a donor egg from two people who have never met, and then that baby is going to grow inside of me. I mean that's pretty crazy shit! I think one of my worries has been what if I give birth – this is obviously if it all works and it all happens – and I look at the child and I go, 'Oh, I don't recognise you,' because it doesn't carry my genes. I'll be looking at my child, imagining what its parents look like. I'm counting a lot on the fact that scientists have done research and it is proven that as the cell is multiplying and it becomes the fetus it's soaking in your chromosomes and your DNA – it's your blood, and it's your spirit – so I think there will be a resemblance somehow, it's just there's a mix of all three of us. And I just think, it's almost like I'm adopting a baby that I've grown.

I have no idea what to expect as a parent. I know that I have got a very big rapport with children. I love kids and kids tend to gravitate towards me, but I suppose one of the things I'm slightly worried about is, will I have the patience for it? Because I'm used to, you know, at 44 years old nearly, doing what I want and when I want. Lying in if I want to, you know, all of those things. So it's kind of the mechanics of it that I worry about. Will I be up to it? Will I be good enough? Will I be able to cope? But I love kids, and I have loads of ideas.

Up until now, like literally, my life has been about work. I have spent all my life working – must work, must work, must earn money, must earn money, how will I look after myself? And then feeling like my life doesn't make any sense because I don't have any children, I don't have a partner, I don't have a family; I'm not doing anything for anybody else. How am I going to make sense of my life? So I think if I have the treatment and it doesn't work, that's probably when I will go, 'Oh my God.' At the end of the day, obviously I'm going to be gutted and disappointed and all the rest of it, but I don't have to have *my* baby. I could quite easily give love to a child that's six and needs a home. I want to be part of a family. I don't want to be just me.

So. I've been meditating, and I'm giving myself three months to do my acupuncture and to do the nutrition thing before I start treatment. You know, I'm going to give it my best shot. That's all I can do. If that spirit's supposed to come, it will come.

Sonja,

55, Lives in New Zealand

I was adopted when I was only a few days old and my mother was about 15 years old. I was really lucky because the parents who adopted me were just fantastic. They were amazingly loving. I was one of five children; I had two older brothers and two older sisters who all went on to have children themselves, so I was the babysitter. I was the person who was there for my nephews and nieces, and they were really close in age to me because my oldest brother's oldest son is just four years younger than me. Looking after children was something that was just part of life really, and I enjoyed it. I always wanted to become a mother myself, but it was never quite the right time for me.

I left New Zealand when I was 25 and I travelled around for a while overseas. I did a year in the US, about two years in Australia and five or six in London. When I was 34 I was in London, and I met my now husband, who was living in Italy.

We met on the internet; this is back in 1996 when it was just booming into being a public place. There was a group of us who used to talk to each other and interact online in a chatroom, but there was no kind of relationship; it was just a place we went to talk to other people with similar interests. It was the days when people could just type away and talk to people, and you had no idea what they looked like but you became friends through conversation. It was great. So he and I were both part of this group and it just so happened that one weekend my husband was coming over to London for a holiday and I said, 'Oh you're welcome to come and sleep on my couch.' It ended up that we became involved, and we had a relationship toing and froing between London and Italy for about a year.

By that stage I was pretty much a career person, working for a big multinational financial services firm. We got married and I thought it would just happen that I would get pregnant; we wouldn't try, but I wasn't on contraception or anything, and if it happened, it happened. I fell pregnant about three months before I was due to move over to Italy. I went into a bit of a panic, and that's when I had my first miscarriage. I moved to Italy, and from then up until I was 40 I had three more miscarriages. I just couldn't carry.

With one of the pregnancies I actually heard the baby's heartbeat. That was amazing! But then when I went back a week later for a ten-week check-up, there was no heartbeat. So I went home and cried, and then we had to prepare to go back the next day and have a D&C. It was the worst experience of my life. I turned up at 7 a.m. and the room was full of all the staff. I walked into the operating room and lay on the bed. My arms were strapped down and my legs were put into stirrups. Then a nurse came along with what I would describe as a bucket and painting brush of antiseptic, and literally just slapped the antiseptic all over the bottom part of me. I'm lying there completely exposed, nothing to help me get over the embarrassment. It was like being on a factory line. They had all these women to do, strap your arms down and slap, slap, slap. Finally I fell asleep thank God, because the humiliation of the whole thing was awful. They knew my circumstances; they knew that I had miscarried. To treat people like that was just dreadful.

I wouldn't say I got depressed, but it did affect me hugely. I could see the chances of having a family and being a mother dwindling, because I was getting older. One of the things I realised was that actually you can't wait to have a career; you've got to just take the dive and go for it if it's what you really want. I hadn't been in a situation to be able to do that though, because I hadn't had a partner. So we kept trying and trying, and then about four years ago I started going through menopause. And that's when it all kind of…the realisation came that that was it. It was devastating. It was all over.

By this point we had moved to New Zealand, and when we'd been here about three or four years we decided we would try to adopt or be foster parents. We went through the training programme, which was a series of three days learning about what it's like, what happens and the rights and so forth. When we finished the course we were assigned a social worker. The options available were fostering, adopting or adopting from overseas, and we were told you have to be extremely lucky to adopt a child in New Zealand – because there just aren't many children up for adoption – so we were looking at Chile because my husband is South American. Because of our ages we couldn't have a child under ten years old, and we would have had to have gone there for three months, which was going to be financially extremely hard for us. So we had to give up that one, and started looking at fostering.

At that stage I was the main income earner and my husband was working from home. We started getting the visits from the social worker that were part of the vetting process for fostering. We passed their scrutiny – 'Yes you seem to have a safe place, and the referees that you've given us speak highly of you' – and then they said, 'So Sonja, when will you give up work?' I told them I wouldn't, because my husband would be at home and he would ensure that the child would go to school, they'd come back, he'd look after them and this is the way it is; this is our plan. And we basically got told that wasn't acceptable, because you can't have a man as the main carer. And that was it. I felt like I'd gone back to God knows where or when. I hate to say it, but I have loathed their social workers ever since.

We were devastated because that was our last opportunity to be parents taken away from us. I was just distraught; they took away my last chance to be a mother. And the thing was, we'd moved back to New Zealand, and it had been a little bit of a struggle to get back up and going again. I have had to really work hard to get to where I am now, and we're in a position where we have a nice lifestyle with disposable income. We have a lovely four bedroom house and spare rooms. And what we ended up with was a cat.

I'm the only person out of my family who doesn't have children; everybody has hordes of kids, and their kids have kids, and I know there's so much that I feel that is missing. My husband is extremely intelligent, and he's a lovely guy who's great with children. Children are just drawn to him. But the opportunity to bring up a child – to teach them and mentor them and give them the love that they may not have – just hasn't been given to us. As much as we love having a life where we do whatever we want to do, it is hard not having a child that you have in the house, someone else that you can care for. Even today I find it really upsetting. I know that when I die and when my husband dies that's it; we have nobody of our own to pass ourselves on to. Mortality issues became very big. What do we do with everything we have?

In the middle of 2016 I was approached by the local school asking if we would be interested in having a homestay student from overseas. So this young girl who was about to turn 18 from Hong Kong came to stay with us for four months. She seemed really lovely. Her parents were over here with her at first, but pretty soon they went back, and then we got this letter saying, 'Oh by the way, we forgot to tell you that she's dyslexic, and she finds socialising difficult sometimes.' I spoke to the school and they didn't know either. She was a girl that was 18 going on 13. You'd give her a hug and it felt really uncomfortable.

She was really sweet, and we had some fun times with her, but we just never got that interaction we were hoping for. We took her on for another year because she wanted to come back, and no one wanted her. But she was under a lot of pressure from her parents because she'd turned 19 and she still hadn't passed any exams; she was very slow, and her parents' expectations of her to go into business were just outrageously high. We found that no matter how much we interacted with her she became withdrawn, because she knew she'd be going back to Hong Kong and she didn't want to go. She spent most of her time in her room, with me trying to draw her out, and interacting with her to try and get her English up. She spent the last three months sitting in her room watching Chinese videos on YouTube. In November I went to a potluck dinner they had at the school with all the other students, and I just sat there thinking, 'Oh my God, everybody else had these great relationships with the students and we had the withdrawn girl.' But the dinner gave me a little bit of hope, and I'd like to try it again.

She's gone back now, and we've tried to communicate but haven't heard anything. We might try it again though, because that's the closest we got. I think if you can make their life a little bit better or a little bit more fun, and they come away with a sense of being wanted or being cared for, then that is worthwhile. I kind of feel thwarted on every level in terms of trying to be a mother. I have an extremely loving husband, but I feel as if I have a huge hole in my life, and I don't think I'll ever really get over it.

I'll keep trying to find a way to give the love I have. And to get used to it somehow.

Claudia,

35, *Lives in Australia*

I can only speak from where I'm at, at the moment, because I'm sure it will go somewhere else next week, or month, or year.

My husband and I had a really tough few years at the beginning of our marriage. We were working through a lot of stuff. So I was 32 when we came to the point where we said, 'Okay, we'll start trying for a baby,' and I was like, 'I'll just get pregnant.'

And I thought I was! There were a few little symptoms, and I googled them, and it looked like I was pregnant, the first time.

I wasn't. And I was like okay, well shit, whatever. And that went on, and it just kept going on month by month like that. You know, every month: 'Am I? Am I? No.' It was just a rollercoaster because you'd get your hopes right up and they'd be dashed. Eventually I started taking pregnancy tests before I got my period because I couldn't handle waiting. After a year we started getting testing. Testing everything.

They called it 'unexplained infertility', which is kind of a frustrating thing, but IVF was an option for me.

Late last year I quit my job. I'm a film producer, and I was at the point where I felt like I needed to take a back step in my career – which was a weird feeling, as a woman, to have – but I wanted to have a child. That was my main focus. It's been my main focus for two years, really, and it's been very difficult. But through it I think I've also learned – you know the hindsight thing – a lot of resilience.

So. I was going to start IVF originally last year, but I thought, 'No, I'll start it in the New Year.' And actually, I'm meant to really start it next week. But I sort of went into this existential kind of – 'crisis' is a strong word – but I started asking all these really big questions about why I was doing this. It got triggered by a film I watched called *Koyaanisqatsi*. It starts off with these special landscapes, and then humans start getting involved, there's more and more people, and they're like parasites on the earth, and they're just destroying the planet. It's a very bleak picture of humanity. And I just started asking myself, 'Why do I so desperately want to contribute to that? To add more? Another person to this world? Like, what it is about me that really wants to do that?'

The main reason I came up with was probably 'purpose'. I'm certainly not discrediting someone who has a child, because I think I would totally do that in a heartbeat, and if I got pregnant I'd have that child and be very happy. But it is quite an obvious way to find purpose. And maybe I have…

a *different* purpose. It's like, the energy that you put into a child, you know, you take that energy and you could put that into something else, whether it's adoption, or charity work, or your career or whatever. Is having a child the best way to fulfil my purpose here, in this short time that I have on earth? I don't know the answers yet, but these are the questions.

In some ways over the last few months I feel like I've been waking up a little bit. Thinking about why I'm doing things. There are all these arguments going around in my head – biological, logical, emotional – but there is a part of me that gets excited about the idea of not having children and what that means. In terms of time, in terms of money, in terms of… like, resources. You know, there's so much need in the world, what could I do?

The biological side of me sways towards wanting to have children, and right now I'm at the place where I'm swinging more towards adoption. If we could adopt that's probably what we would prefer to do over IVF, because IVF is like you're forcing a thing to happen. And even if I did it, it may not work. So at this stage I'm leaning towards not doing it, I guess. But there's that question of whether I would regret it in the future. Would my husband regret not trying? I think what scares me the most about IVF is doing it and it not working – which part of me feels like it might.

Or even…what if we didn't have children at all? And that scares me. It's a new road. It feels like you'd get a lot of pity. I understand that pity, because it's like you've lost someone who you've never met; as though there's this amazing person who you could create, potentially, and you are *longing* for. It's actually a person, and you'll maybe never get to meet that person. So, it's like a loss for something that you've never had, or someone you've never met. I especially feel the loss when I get my period. You know, where you get the bleeding, and of course you haven't lost someone, but you've lost a hope. A possibility.

Late last year I went to a concert with my husband. It was quite powerful music, very cinematic, and I just kind of got lost in my thoughts. Suddenly I had this very strong visualization of a little baby boy. I could picture what he looked like, and his black curly hair, and I was holding him. It was a really strong image that's still with me. I still sometimes think about it, and think, 'That's our son.' I don't know where it came from, and I'm not necessarily saying it's a premonition, but it felt really nice. Like it was an actually physical person I could see and visualize. I sort of felt like that's our baby, you know? Like it was this beautiful creation between us both.

And there are moments like last night, when I woke up with this really intense sadness. I was feeling…feeling loss. And I was thinking to myself – because it's a weird situation – I've never lost someone very close to me, and when you lose someone you don't have a choice, whether you lose them or not. Whereas I'm in a situation where I do have a choice as to whether I lose that person or not. I felt a sense of sadness and loss, but then a sense of having a choice, which made it harder in some ways.

But in another way it made me go, 'Well, yeah; if you

decide to take one path you're going say goodbye to another.' It's that thing of when you're trying to decide between two things; you don't want to miss out on something, but you are going to miss out on *something*, because if you have a child you're probably going to miss out on career stuff and other opportunities to help people. And travel. You know? But at the same time if I don't have a child then I'm going miss out on that magical experience that no one can know until they've done it, of having a child. And it's like, is it worth it? I don't know. You can't know.

Louise,

40, *Lives in New Zealand*

Right through my teens and 20s and 30s I felt the biological clock *ticking* so strongly. Tick, tick, *ticking*. I really identified with being a mum, and I was geared up for that. I already had a name for my child; I'd heard my neighbour talking to a young child and he used her name. *Silvie*. I knew in that moment that was the name that I would call my daughter. It still brings tears to my eyes to think of it now.

But I never met anyone to have a child with. I had relationships through my 20s, but they were all short term. In my 30s I stopped even meeting anyone and that was such a big component to starting a family. I felt a desperate need for a relationship and to be a mum – above everything, to be a mum – and it just got more and more unbearable that it wasn't happening for me. It was *so* painful. Such agony. Why not me? Why not *me*? It was so hard to fathom. I was in cycles of getting darker and darker, and each time I became more weighed down by despair. Not being able to express myself as a mother became heartbreaking and overwhelming.

When I got to 37, it all just got too much: the desire, the longing for a child, not being met. I really had to face it and make a choice about where I was going to sit with it.

I had sooooo much therapy. It was very helpful at the time, but I was in a loop, going around in circles. I was trying to resolve the situation, but it was never being resolved because I didn't have a baby in my arms. So I would feel better for a while, and then I would be back to this heartache and these thoughts, and I would be seeking support again.

Finally it got so dark it scared me. It made me feel that I didn't want to be here. It was more than just the thought of not wanting to live, and it *really* frightened me.

I was living by the sea at the time, and one day I was going for a walk on the track around the cliff along the sea. I can see myself there now. I was in that spiralling darkness, and then something happened. Something, I don't know what – grace? – enabled me to just…turn. I recognized it. Something like an epiphany maybe. I had no choice but to just turn around.

I think what happened was that my desire for peace became stronger than my desire to have a child. It became a mantra, almost: 'I just want inner peace. I want inner peace.' After that time I still would go in spirals a little bit, but it's never been dark like that again. I started to feel more supported by life, after feeling for so long like I wasn't, because I wasn't being given what I wanted. And I started to feel greater peace.

Now I feel I just wasn't *meant* to be a mother. And I have

such faith in everything being as it's meant to be. It's something that really struck me, so profoundly, when I had turned around from the darkness and back to the light: this really clear realization that I wasn't meant to be a mum. It just dawned on me, and blew me away, because I had put everything into assuming that I was. I'd never thought I wouldn't be.

Something that really helped – and this was just over a year ago – was that I went to see a therapist that I've seen off and on, and he said, 'You have options.' He suggested I could look into fostering or adopting, or fertility treatment – doing IVF with a donor and having a child on my own. I felt I could totally do that – I never felt I couldn't be a solo mum – and I felt really empowered. But when I realized that I *could*, something also started to awaken in me, and I realised there just wasn't an impulse to do it. I began to feel that actually I don't have to take that step, that I don't want to be raising teenagers in my 50s. I want to be winding down and thinking about what I want to do when I retire! So that was another big settling time, another part of the puzzle of finding peace.

These days I work with little ones in a preschool. I just adore babies. I love babies so, so much! And I was laughing recently because I thought, 'All I ever wanted was a baby,' and now I have *nine*, every day! I remember on Mother's Day a few years ago I was like, 'Happy Mother's Day to me!' I really feel I am mothering, in a way. I know it's not the same – and I can't know the difference, because I'm not a mum – but I feel like it's the same part of my heart that holds these infants and toddlers.

I never, never knew that peace could come through that, and I feel lucky in that way. It feels like a rich experience, that I have found a way of coming back into the light. Since then, since the darkness, maybe I've looped back a little bit, but I don't think I will ever go back. I know the way back now, because I took the road through the dark. Now it's illuminated; it's easy to come back up the road. Like I said, the peace is too important.

It felt really, really, *really* good to turn 40. I've accepted so much, and it feels liberating. Life gets better with age.

Hannah,

45, Lives in Spain

I was brought up as a boy, in a hyper-masculine environment in England. I went to a preparatory boys' school and then to a predominantly male secondary. My experience of femininity was almost non-existent until I went abroad, when I went to my first co-ed high school. It was a complete revelation in every sense; up until then, puberty was a period of immense shutdown.

I didn't think about having children, growing up. I was in a school full of bankers' families and people who were likely to go off into the city and do those sorts of jobs. The unwritten narrative for me in that environment was that you made women have kids, and they went off, and you did your successful career and paid for them. There was no discussion at any point academically or socially – even amongst the female staff who taught us – of any kind of thought about growing up to be a respectful male towards women and sharing the burden of childcare. That was off the radar.

I had a good group of friends. I was in the artistic side of that group – the more effeminate side – and as androgynous as I could reasonably get away with without being considered weird. My set of people was musician-type boys who were pretty feminine, especially when compared to others who were obviously very much into rugby and all that stuff. But we never ever discussed things like children or having our own kids.

From my perspective as a trans woman I've come to have a very profound appreciation of the commonalities of the human body that biological males and biological females share. Just by reprogramming the endocrine system chemically, I'm able to become – to all intents and purposes – biologically female: a woman. My sense of the world becomes feminine. When I transitioned it gave 'permission' chemically for my natural brain – which was born female in terms of its wiring and the way it wants to think and feel about the world – to align with my body. The endocrine system allows me to feel more sensually; my nerve endings are literally more sensitive.

I've become a lot more maternal – a lot more clucky. It's part of my body aligning more with my feelings, and my brain, my thought processes and my vision of the world. Like I'll walk past a kid in the street and immediately I feel 'Awwww'. I'll want to hug it, and give it a kiss, and embrace the joy of it. I think that's a special thing that women have and understand between themselves: this joy of bringing this new life into the world and watching it grow. It's a delight in children. They're not just a means to generate the next generation of bankers or whoever; there's something much more spiritual going on with that, much more wondrous. It's made me appreciate the extraordinary kaleidoscopic journey that women have.

Speaking from having experienced the world chemically in both senses, I think women are designed to be in general more sensitive to the needs of children, to pick up more empathetically to what their needs are. And perhaps to simply notice things. It's a different way of being and it's not just about social conditioning; it goes deeper than that I think, much deeper.

As I've felt as my body became more inhabited fundamentally with a female sensoriness, I've wondered how many years it's going to be before somebody who feels as I do will be able to be blessed with the option of carrying a child themselves, and really fixing the great thing that we can't fix. I wish that I had had a womb. I wish that I had had the opportunity to have children myself, to experience the pain of everything that's bad about it, enduring all the things that make up the blessing of being able to have children yourself and experience that. I can only imagine it. I'm a creative person and I'm pretty good at imagining things, but there's a sadness that it can't physically happen to me. Amongst all the things that I am happy and feel blessed for, it's a powerful sadness.

The times when I feel the most sad about not having had children I think is when I'm around my stepdaughter. She's my ex's daughter, and we were together for six years. I have in one sense been lucky; I've sort of brought up a child from an early age and she's now coming up to 12 at the end of the year – so a formative chunk of time. It wasn't easy for me because I was very shut down before but I grew to really understand the joy of parenting and now – through having transitioned – it's much, much easier to have far more bandwidth to give myself permission to just let go and enjoy it. I miss her hugely. I miss reading her stories, I miss lying with her so she'd go to sleep, all that stuff; it's really difficult not having her in my life.

I saw her briefly one Sunday, and she came down the stairs and just hugged me for a minute and didn't say anything, and what can you do? I feel like that really tears me apart because I'm not a daily part of her life anymore. She never questioned, and immediately accepted my need to change from being a step-parent – who she perceived to be as a stepdad – to a stepmother. She got it in ten minutes, and she's never misgendered me again. She always calls me Hannah, and she always hugs me as if I am another mum. She actually said, 'I've got two mums.'

I feel like I'm circumstantially childless, and in that sense no different from other women who find themselves in that situation for any one of a number of medical reasons that women in their early 40s experience. I had a medical reason for not having children; it wasn't spiritual, and it wasn't anything to do with my mental health. It's a physical impediment to being able to do certain things in the world. I think if I try and talk through that experience and put it out there from a trans perspective, it is really hard. I don't claim – or want – to speak for the trans community, but I have become aware that it's not just me; it seems to be quite a common thread. Of course there's variation as with any group of people, and there are some people who are fine with not having children. And some of my sisters will have had kids biologically with a woman, but for me that never felt like my path.

I think that many aspects of my character were released when I transitioned and was able to be fully alive, and to be seen by people as my identity that I knew was me, inside. There were many things that suddenly I felt I had the freedom to do and not be regarded as misgendered. I had this huge buried wadge of wanting to mother: to be caring, to be compassionate, to share that with people, nurturing, protecting. Those were qualities that I had not been encouraged to develop in the same kind of way.

A couple of weeks ago I randomly came across people in a women's group online discussing adoption and their particular reasons for needing to adopt – 'I'm in my 40s' or whatever – and it just brought it home to me that you can come from different pathways to reaching this point in your life as a woman that you cannot have your own child. It made me think, 'Well that's a possibility for me; mothering could be part of my future.' So I'm not shutting down that possibility at all, but I'm 45 and my career suffered greatly because of my dysphoria. I'm only now adjusting and really able to thrive in my chosen career, and I feel like I've got a lot of ground to make up. And that's not just a completely selfish thing; if I am seriously going to look to adopt a child and give it a good life and cherish it as a mother, then I'd better be able to have a stable income and profession to make that work as a single person. Somebody very nicely said to me once, 'You know, you'd make a really good mum,' so I thought, 'We'll see.' I don't know whether it will happen but I do think it would be something I would find extraordinarily fulfilling and of course – like every other woman – very challenging.

As another way of doing mothering I think I will try to find ways of supporting children in the world. For example, in the new business I'm putting together I went to an open day run by professional women, for girls who are in their teenage years in high school and considering career options. Just for girls – to let them know that there was more for them than marrying and having kids. A thousand girls turned up, and there were women around to talk about all sorts of careers. I was there with my stall, and I got a surprising number of girls who were interested in and wanting to find out about music technology. It occurred to me that perhaps having an ability to teach young women to be able to do this particular kind of thing would be something that I could do. I'd like to be able to be around children in some way as a kind of motherly guiding figure, to do something that's positive for them. Not exclusively for girls, but I think girls generally have some catching up to do in terms of some industries with technology: music technology and engineering jobs. They're very, very good at them when they do them; they often excel.

Manifesting that mothering instinct in ways that are beneficial to the community is very fulfilling and satisfying for me. It's a new experience, but something I really like the feel of.

And it helps me to realise that there are many, many cisgender women who haven't been able to have children, and who have found also a way to give an outlet to the way they feel by doing a different kind of mothering.

Maree,

33, Lives in New Zealand

I was always seen in my family as being quite a tomboy. Even from my teens I was interested in the work that I wanted to do – working with people, helping people somehow – and early on I embarked on training to establish the foundation for a career. In my mid- to late 20s my study really got underway and that became my focus; that was my baby so to speak. I was pouring all my creative energy into that.

When I finished my degree a couple of years ago, I decided to take a year off and go travelling, and while I was overseas a big thing happened. I met someone and accidentally got pregnant. The father wasn't someone I could imagine being with and raising a child together, and he was on the other side of the world. It all felt completely wrong and I knew really, really quickly what I needed to do. I rushed home to have a termination.

I came home as soon as I found out I was pregnant, but when I got here I was put on a waiting list for the procedure, and I was literally waiting for weeks. By the time it happened I was actually nine and a half weeks, and all sorts of things were happening to my body. I'm not a person who can pretend something's not happening, so I was processing it all during the whole experience. I was kind of connecting to this little embryo and apologising that I just can't do this. I explained to it, you know, that I did love it and care for it, and that it was the best thing for it not to come this time round. In the end I felt that was supposed to happen to me at that time. I made peace with the whole experience and with the embryo, and I believe now that if that soul was supposed to be with me, it will find its way back at some stage.

Somehow though, it did something to me. Something changed. That maternal thing – that wasn't there before – came. I'm not sure what happened, whether it's like a human instinct thing or some biochemical hormonal change just from being pregnant for a short time. I began to feel really differently about wanting to have a child.

My sister's got four children. She's older than me, and she started when she was 21. She always just wanted to be a mum; she loves having babies and growing them. I find it a bit rough being around her family sometimes, because they're all nested in and they're this really awesome solid family. They've got their own little cool family culture happening and yeah, that can be a bit rough sometimes. I notice how guarded I am around them, and because I am such a maternal, nurturing person it doesn't make sense for me not to be completely that way around her children. I tend to not see them as often as I could.

I notice the same response with my cousin too. He lives at the other end of the country and he's like a brother to me, a younger brother. In the last two years he's met this awesome girl. They fell completely head over heels in love, got married and had a baby, really quickly. And they're perfect; it's just lovely. I'm so happy for them and just thinking about their situation makes me smile, you know? But I've noticed that when I'm physically around them it's beautiful to watch, but I fall really flat when I come home. It takes me a few days to pick myself back up again. The first time for about three days I was thinking, 'What's going on here?' and then I recognised that it's obviously something I really, really want. So while I'm super happy for them, I feel quite sad. Like I'm missing out on all that, because it's right in front of me and they're so happy.

In terms of the legitimacy of grieving for not having a child though, it's difficult. I had the opportunity to have a child, so I don't have the right to be sad about not having children. I give myself the right, privately. But I can understand that in society's eyes it seems logical – looking from the outside in – that if a woman had the opportunity to have a child and didn't, and then was sad about not having children, that wouldn't make much sense.

To me, being a mother means being really nurturing. It's almost part of the human experience, and if I don't get to experience it I'll feel like I've missed out on a really important part of being human. There is a little bit of a void there. My life is rich in so many ways and I love all other aspects of it, but there's nothing that I can give my maternal nurturing-ness to.

So I'm aware of these little pangs of feelings that come up periodically, but other than that I'm not completely clear on exactly how I feel about it all. I'm usually really self-aware of what's going on with my own stuff and process things quite quickly, but because this isn't something that I really talk about with anyone, it's left semi unprocessed and in the background. There's no label or box or term for it to fit in. It's too painful to keep at the front with everyday life, so I pack it back there somewhere. It's like a semiconscious decision to keep it back there, but I don't know how useful it would be to bring it forward, because there's nothing I can do about it. But it's still there. I think I pay a price for packing it away: being overweight. I comfort eat.

I've always been open to adoption or fostering. I'd like to have the opportunity to nurture, to try to give someone all that they need. I'm hoping to meet someone that I can team up with and who wants to parent as much as I do and look at our options together. I don't know if they exist; I'd say the chances are 50/50. I'd like to be underway by 35, 36. Looking long term I see the child having a mum and a dad that are not too old; I'd like to be quite active and have fun and, and not be too decrepit with my children!

Worst case scenario?... Well, I'll just go and buy some land and set up a farmlet and have a multitude of animals. And set up a retreat for people. I guess it's Plan B.

Julia,

48, Lives in New Zealand

I grew up in the 1970s and second wave feminism was just starting. When I came across it at 17 I was really influenced by the extreme end of it, and I was a bit anti-men for a while. At that age I didn't have the capacity to realize that I needed to be able to *live* with men because I'm a heterosexual woman. I thought that was the life my mother had, and I rejected it. But I remember at some point – in my mid- to late 30s – thinking, 'Oh, bloody feminism! It never did me any good! Look! I'm childless!'

I'm one of four children, and I always imagined becoming a mother, but I was ambivalent about having children in my early adult years. I was over-responsible as the oldest child and I couldn't wait to get away. In some ways I didn't want the responsibility of being a mother myself. Plus, as I grew up... well, basically I was surrounded by dead babies. My mother had two miscarriages and two stillborns and I was the oldest. I sometimes wonder if that's actually had an influence at a really deep level, knowing motherhood to be perilous. In some ways it terrified me.

I actually did get pregnant twice in my 20s and had two terminations, so it's not like I couldn't have babies. I just felt too young. And I think it probably felt like there was a lot more opportunity, like this is not going to be my only chance.

I've often wondered what decision I would have made if I'd known then what I know now, and I don't have an easy answer for that. I deeply regret those decisions, but I don't know if I'd do it any differently. Thinking about it now, I'd still make that same decision – given the person I was in my 20s – but I don't think I would have in my 30s. When I think about the idea of 'choice', and the choices I made, yes I made a conscious choice not to have two children but I don't believe that I have ever said, 'I'm not having children.' That wasn't a choice. It was like a constellation of circumstances that didn't allow for it to happen. It's horrible really.

So, when the opportunities were there I chose not to, and then when I reached my early 30s the biological clock really seemed to kick in and I wanted to have children. I think I thought, 'There's still time,' but I was in and out of relationships. I was deluded in some respects. There are all these people round me having babies and I'm still going, 'Oh yeah. It will happen. One day.' I wasn't really conscious of time passing and conscious that actually, if you want this, you have to make it happen in some way. You have to be active about it, and I guess I wasn't. I was probably a little bit more passive, until it was too late.

I remember early on someone saying to me, 'Maybe children – as spirits – choose their own time.' I remember when I first heard that I thought, 'What a load of shit. What a load of shit!' I really wasn't ready to hear that. But over the years, I've found myself wondering, and I suppose I do believe that to some degree. It was just the wrong time for them, and perhaps they might come back. They might come back. It feels like a comfort strategy to say that in some respects but…I just don't know. I have a very clear understanding now of why I didn't have the capacity to choose to have those children; at the time it just didn't feel right. So I suppose there has had to be a process of forgiving myself, because I had the opportunities to do it. And you know, love takes many forms and being an aunt is one of those forms. At another level, maybe these spirits do choose; maybe that was their time and it wasn't meant to be that they could fully incarnate. They could only get that far, whatever that means.

As I've got older I've always thought about the two children that I didn't have, and wondered what they would look like and what they would be doing. And I notice myself attracted to children of the same age; I think, 'Oh they'd be this age now; oh that would be cool.' It's like they *have* grown up with me.

It's a very painful process grieving for not having a child, and adapting to a different life. For me it was eased in a very personal way. I live in New Zealand, and three years ago, as part of my professional development as a psychotherapist, I did a Māori healing course. After many months of training, my teacher said, 'Julia, the spirits of your children are not at rest, and they need to be taken to rest.' We discussed what that meant and what it involved, and where and how I would do it. Usually in Māori terms it means going to a *marae* or a family plot but I'm not Māori and my family doesn't have that, so I chose a location in the mountains in the South Island. I invited a friend along and I collected all these little *taonga*[1] for them, and I went up into the mountains and did a ritual. In that process I really claimed being a mother, and I put them to rest.

So now I know where they are...and whenever I drive through that area I cry and I talk to them. It was very hard, but I've done what I think a mother should do, which is to take care of them. One of the meanings I take from all of that is, yes, I *am* a mother, although I don't have children. But I'm not very visible with that knowledge, as far as the rest of the world goes. I haven't yet had the courage to talk about myself in that way with others, and I certainly don't talk about it to my family.

It was probably menopause that finally made me realize it wasn't going to happen. I remember thinking, 'It's not over until then! It's really not over until then!' And even then there was an element of denial, like, 'People get pregnant in menopause! It could still happen!' But I think that on another level the question began to arise in my mind: would I actually want to be an old mother? If the opportunity arose say two or three years ago, probably the answer would have been 'yes', but I didn't meet anyone that I was willing to do it with.

Dealing with other people's responses to my not having

---

1   Treasures.

a child is something I find really hard. I have come to quite a good place emotionally about not having children, but I haven't quite mastered the interpersonal, social settings, and the dread of being judged about it gets me every time. I live in terror of people asking me, 'Do you have children?' I just don't know what they think, and I'm afraid they might judge me as a failure somehow.

And there isn't a recognized category for people in my situation. There's a marginalization I think, and I begin to understand more what it's like to be a minority. I mean, yes I'm white, middle class, and there's lots of privileges from that, but what I've noticed as I've got older is that society is geared to families. Politically, or in the media, or you know – you fill out a form and there's no place for me on that form as far as I can see. I look at it and think, 'Hmm. Where's my experience there?' It's hard to find an identity that fits.

I do feel a sense of grief and regret about not having the experience of being pregnant and breastfeeding. And the grief is also about not having something. I remember – probably in my early 40s – reading about people being grandparents, and having a huge amount of grief then. I'm not going to be a grandmother either! When you make the decision not to have a child, you don't know the impact of that decision. You just don't know. You don't know that it's going to take away all of these opportunities or experiences.

So it continues to be a loss. You lose family. You lose the experience of loving in a particular way, being required to love in a particular way. You lose the opportunity to know yourself better, I think, as a person.

I've really consciously chosen to use the phrase 'childfree' now, rather than 'childless'. I guess child*less* seems for me that I'm *less* than, because I'm without child, and I definitely rebel against that idea; that makes me very, very angry, that I might be perceived to be that. And because I now think, well, okay, I *am* free in a sense! I keep reminding myself of what's possible in a childfree, rather than a childless, condition. And that sits alongside the regret, which is definitely there, but it's a lot less than it used to be.

Raewyn,

47, *Lives in India*

I don't know how to enter this story.

I always aspired to marrying and having children. I still aspire to get married but I'm 47 now. I'm in the middle of three girls in my family. My sisters both married when they were in their really early 20s, and had children in their late 20s, early 30s. I always expected that I'd meet someone and have children like them, but I had some trauma in my teens that really impacted me badly and it was not processed at the time. It meant that I was very afraid of men, in my 20s especially.

It wasn't any one thing, but a really horrible series of events that happened during my teens and early 20s. When I was in my early teens a guy exposed himself to me, at a public event, in a public space. It happened a couple of times. I remember feeling really powerless and shocked by that. Another time a family friend – who was staying in our home – made sexual advances towards me. He didn't follow through and I never told my parents, but I think it generated a wariness in me.

Then when I was 16 my father died suddenly. The shock of that separation and loss at a quite a formative stage…it left me with a sense of abandonment and not being safe in the world.

Then just before my 19th birthday I was working in a job where I did really early shifts, starting at 4 a.m. I'd gone out on a date with a guy and then came back to the house I was living in. There were other people in the house and because I had to get up early, I'd just gone to bed. I don't know whether I was absolutely exhausted, or whether he had drugged me, but I woke up and he was on top of me, penetrating me. Luckily there was someone in the house, and I was able to threaten him to get away or I would scream, and he left.

I don't know that he was able to enter into me, but I'm never sure; the next day I was so sore. But the trauma of that was the most horrific thing in terms of impact. For years and years – probably for close to 12, 13 years after that – I couldn't sleep properly at night if there was no one else in the house. I went to the doctor just to have a physical check, but I was young; I didn't recognise the psychological impact. People didn't talk much about trauma in those days. My approach to dating really changed at that point. I became very wary, and almost a little frozen and hypersensitive. I started to develop some post-traumatic stress disorder (PTSD) symptoms, but I didn't recognize them.

Then a couple of years later I was just starting out on my first teaching job, out in a small country school. I was in a house on my own – which was already scary for me because of what had happened – and I heard rustling noises outside my bedroom window. It was dark outside and I thought it was an animal so I just walked outside and right there, not more than three or four metres away from me, was a man standing in the bushes outside my window. I yelled my head off; there was a broomstick on the veranda and I grabbed it and held it like a softball bat, and I just yelled and yelled and yelled. He fled around the side of the house, but then I didn't know if I was safe. Was he going to come into the house and attack me? I went inside the house and locked the doors. And luckily, the phone had just been connected – honestly like an hour or two hours beforehand – and I was able to phone the police. They came round and I went and stayed with another teacher. I was already fearful because of what had happened previously, and this triggered more fear. And then, because the police got involved, they wanted to find out who this man was. It ended up that a detective picked me up one day and took me downtown. He said, 'If you see the man just tell me,' and I pointed him out. They arrested him and it went to court, and then one morning I got up and on the windshield of my car there was a note: 'You fucking bitch. Withdraw the charges or you'll die.' I was terrified. I didn't withdraw, and it went to court, and when I had to testify, he was sitting there in front of me. And he started to abuse me, in court, as I was testifying.

Around then I started to get chronic stomach pains. I guess it became psychosomatic because I was so stressed. That job was the start of a two-year teaching service and I lived in this heightened state of fear for the whole two years. The man was still around in the community; I taught his grandchildren at the school. I was afraid of him, but I also had a more generalised fear of all men. I began to get bad PTSD symptoms that really affected my body. When the two years were up I left and went back to the city to another job. But I was carrying all this stress and my body just collapsed with adrenal fatigue. I was 27, and I couldn't work at all for ten months I was so sick.

There was one last thing. When I was 14 I had a boyfriend. He lived a little while away, but he was my first love. He was part Māori and we carried on dating on and off while I was at uni. Around that time he was attacked by white skinheads, and he developed some mental health issues after that. In his mid-20s he committed suicide and for me, we were still...we were best friends. I remember the grief being so much when I heard about that. I just couldn't stop crying, I carried so much grief and I didn't understand, but that was the last of that series of terrible things that had happened for me. I think the grief for him was just actually a culmination of the grief for all the things that had happened.

In my early 30s I went to a counsellor who was able to help me with what had happened. I began to heal, but I didn't start dating again until my mid- to late 30s. I had two long-term relationships, but they didn't work. It just never really happened for me. I think vulnerability was a big part of it: my lack of the ability to be emotionally vulnerable.

I remember in my late 20s and early 30s thinking that I didn't feel particularly maternal but I didn't understand why. Looking back, it's interesting that vocationally I was really engaged in maternal activities at that time. I was working as a teacher in alternative education with young people who were from very vulnerable backgrounds, people who were carrying quite a lot of trauma themselves. A lot of them were from extremely vulnerable and broken families: young people who were being abused in multiple different ways. At that time I carried their burdens in an unhealthy way. I got too involved; my boundaries were really messed up. I think I was loving them maternally, and so during that time – in my late 20s, early 30s – maybe my maternal instincts were being met in that way, so I didn't recognise that need. But later – in my mid- to late 30s – I definitely went through a period of grieving. It feels like it's been my lifetime as an adult grieving for being childless, but I think it was especially at that time during my late 30s and early 40s that I really carried it most. Loss of a dream, loss of what it might have been.

I love nurturing young people – seeing them thrive and realise their potential – and there's something that feels maternally nurturing within that, but it takes shape in different ways. Around that time in my early 40s I thought I had love to give to someone, and I decided to do some respite foster care. I thought children would be easier but quite quickly it was obvious that I 'get' teenagers, so I ended up providing respite care for a girl in her teens. She came to me pretty much every holiday and some weekends, for about four or five years. I just journeyed with her and loved her, and I still do. The hardest thing about coming here to India was leaving her, but I recognised there are a lot of other people in her life that love her. I just knew intuitively that she'll be okay, and we're still in touch regularly from over here.

So I was doing foster care and I thought I would look at doing permanent care instead of respite care. But that was at the time I was starting to think more about vulnerable girls, learning more about human trafficking and sex trafficking. I came over here to India and had a look at the work this organisation is doing, and I just knew within days that this – not India, and not even working overseas – but this area, is something that I wanted to give a significant part of my life to. I was hoping that could be through awareness raising or education in Australia, and not moving overseas because I didn't want to go. But then I realised I wasn't comfortable in Australia anymore either. I kind of wrestled with it for about nine months, and in the end I just recognised that spending some time over here was going to be good, and so that's how I came here, to Mumbai.

It's hard to put into words what it's been like; it's crazy, beautiful, extremely fulfilling, infuriating and frustrating. I think the challenge is living in the heart of a city, in an area that is extremely overpopulated and noisy and smelly and dirty and surrounded by quite a lot of poverty. I'm not a city girl at heart, so there's that challenge. I'm growing slowly to appreciate the place and the work is extremely fulfilling. It feels totally right; it's such a great fit for my passion for justice and with my skillset.

My job is in a really large organisation that works with women who have either been trafficked into the sex trade, or are at risk of being trafficked. We do both prevention and intervention work, and my role is not usually relating to the women in the community or women employed, but in providing education and training for those who are. We work across business and community development, and we're focusing on leadership training to upskill leaders to deliver quality training in a structured, sustainable way. I love seeing people grow and flourish and thrive in their potential; that's really what drives me. My role now is more facilitation, coordination, strategic development and administration, and I get the chance to work with a small number of nationals who are young adults in their 20s. I love encouraging them and seeing them equipped and inspired to carry out their role and find their place. I don't know whether that's particularly maternal, or if it's more nurturing in a greater sense. I think my maternal desire is…I wouldn't say it's fulfilled here, and maybe it's not a strong a need in me anymore. I don't know, I'm not sure; I would say it has shifted in the last few years.

There are times when I am still deeply moved by the most vulnerable here: the children and actually animals as well. I've had to compartmentalise in order to survive I think. You can't take in everything you see and process it, because it's just overwhelming. At the moment my focus is on my work, and in my personal life it's about learning what it means to thrive here, because last year – my first here – was about survival. I want to know what it means for me to thrive in a place like this. I don't have answers yet – plus my work is enough – but if I did do something else here it would be in education. Children.

There are some amazing projects just waiting to happen, and I just have to not look at them! I see the vulnerability, but also the beauty and curiosity of young children to learn and to be safe. I've kind of put that on hold.

I think my passion for justice was there before those difficult experiences in my life happened, but they certainly shaped things for me. When we were growing up as kids we lived in a big old sprawling house, and we often had people come and stay who were really broken in some way. My Dad always had a real heart for justice and I think I was really influenced by him the most. My Mum was a very compassionate lady but from more of a personal perspective; his was probably more ideological, social and political.

So, mine is a sad story, and it's not often I get to tell it, because you can't tell it in its partiality; it only makes sense in the fullness of it. I recognised probably in my 30s that we have a choice about suffering. You know: shit things happen and it's how we respond that matters. I do carry scars, but I don't want them to continue to have a hold on defining how I am in relationship to others. I continue to seek some kind of wholeness, an emotional vulnerability to being open to the possibility of being in intimate loving relationships.

The scars continue to inhibit that a little bit, but in the last two years I feel like I'm more emotionally healthy than I've ever been before. I feel more able to be me, and it feels really good. I see the grand narratives – and also the small narratives – of life. I'm learning about spirituality and emotionality and how the two connect: how we relate to others, how we carry suffering, how we show compassion. People's stories and how they form. And in all of that I can see why I never was able to marry, to commit and have children. I think that's how it all came about for me.

I just look forward to getting older, I really do! Every year I feel like my life gets better.

Genevieve,

45, Lives in England

My mother is a 1970s feminist and her primary message was, 'Educate yourself; you don't want to have to rely on a man. Don't worry about making me a grandmother.' I suspect some of that was her frustration at her own situation for a bright person, but I'm still grateful because it has enabled me to do so much with my life.

I was the first person in my family to go to university and I loved it. I absolutely gobbled it up! At that time my friends were starting to have babies, and if I'm really honest, back then I looked down on them a bit. I used to sing that song to myself by The Specials that went something like, 'You're too young, you're much too young, you should be out having fun.' I love kids – they're fun, they're amazing, they're brilliant – but I thought my friends had wasted themselves.

Then when I got to about 28 I had a period of depression. I was working in a busy big hospital, and a lot of those wards are full of elderly people dying. I saw a lot of poverty:

people who would be living in one room, only heating one room. Most of them couldn't manage the stairs anymore, but their children didn't want them to sell their properties and move somewhere more suitable because that was their inheritance. And they didn't want to either; they were desperate. My job as an occupational therapist was to try and get them home for as long as possible, and to have the best quality of life that they could. I think it was the first time I started to think about death and dying, and it was really shocking.

Luckily I recognised the clinical signs for depression in myself and I found a really good talking therapist. But I knew that if I'd had one period of depression it increased my chances of having another, and that started to colour my thoughts about having a family. I was worried about the moral and ethical responsibility and weight of potentially passing something that had been so profoundly painful for me, onto my children. Would I bring another person into the world knowing that they may have that level of terrible pain?

I'd never had a maternal urge, but as I came out of that period of depression and moved into my early 30s I did. For the first time ever I felt a quickening. And I started to feel as if I was weird: a loser, a leftover woman. Everyone was doing something different from me – being married, having children – and it occurred to me that while I used to look down on those people, actually they seemed to have a nice life. They seemed quite happy! I started to wonder whether the boot was on the other foot, and they looked down on *me*. Maybe they'd had a good thing all along that I had just missed. I felt there was something I didn't get, that everyone else instinctively understood: how to have a relationship with a reasonable normal person and have children.

So I did what has always helped me at times of crisis: I went back into therapy to explore this whole concept of motherhood and what it meant to me, the ambivalence and the struggle, and why I wasn't able to have what I felt was a normal relationship. I'd had a string of boyfriends up until that stage, but I don't ever remember thinking, 'You'd be a great dad!' I realised I needed to do things differently.

At 36 I did online dating and I was lucky enough to meet my current partner, who astonishingly didn't have any mental health problems, any drug or alcohol problems, and just seemed a really normal, reasonable person! By then I had a sense that time was really running out and I was very focused. On my second date with him I said, 'Look I'm going to cut to the chase. I'm not that worried about getting married but I'd really like someone to have a family with,' and luckily it's what he had always wanted as well. We went out together for a year and then I moved in with him, and within about four months of moving in we started trying. It was a wonderful thing to be with someone who I was in love with, this lovely French man who cooked me fantastic food, had dogs, lived in the countryside and really wanted children! It was great, except then it turned out to be not great because it all very quickly became a descent into hell.

The first time I got pregnant we were floating on cloud nine, ecstatically happy. I told my family and my friends and everyone was overjoyed. When I went for my first scan I went by myself, and I remember feeling all happy and sunny, but a few minutes into the scan the staff just went really quiet. There was a pause, and the pause got a bit longer, and then they said they couldn't find a heartbeat.

I just wasn't expecting it. I knew having a miscarriage was a chance, but it's a small chance; I mean, you're more than likely to have a successful pregnancy than to have a miscarriage. I didn't believe them. I didn't *want* to believe them. And then I had to go phone my partner. That was the hardest bit; he was at work in a big office, we were both crying, and I was alone at the clinic. They had a separate room on the side which was the bad news room, so you didn't have to go back into the waiting room with all the other people with big pregnant bellies and young children and fathers looking really happy. That was a godsend, that little room.

Over the next three years I got pregnant three times – one pregnancy a year – but I never got past nine weeks. I had three miscarriages, and all of them have now turned into a family: my imaginary family inside my head. In a way it has helped my grief to imagine what my children would have been like. I still sometimes get asked, 'Do you have children?' and it's always such a difficult question to answer. It's never felt right to say, 'None.' How do I even begin to explain that I have three children, but they're dead? On some level I am a mother; I was their mother for those tiny lives, for that tiny period of time, but on a day-to-day level I don't feel like part of the mother clan or the mother group. I'm a secret mother with an invisible clan.

Everything became torture for those three years. Everywhere I went it was a constant battle, and I couldn't get away. I was hiding in toilets, crying at work when people got pregnant and had baby showers. I remember I would feel like I was being physically punched. And I was having panic attacks at home in the bathroom because I'd had miscarriages there. It felt like there was no reprieve, no end, just like this awful, constant reminder of my failure. I apologised to my partner every day for three years because I thought it was all my fault.

Stopping blaming myself has been profound. One day at the end of that time I heard Jody Day talking about Gateway Women on the radio: this very reasonable, intelligent woman articulating part of what is inside of me, on Radio 4, which gave it immediate credibility because if she was really weird and odd and a crazy old cat lady, they wouldn't let her on Radio 4. After hearing her it took another six months of me feeling awful to get to the point where I thought, 'I've got to go towards the childlessness thing, look over the precipice and jump right into it. This is my life; it's fucking awful, it's not what I wanted, and I don't know how I'm going to get through it.'

Childlessness is such a profound life; it unravels gradually, because you can't know all of what it really means immediately. I have had to reorientate my relationship to myself, to be much more loving and supportive and nurturing to myself, to go, 'You poor thing Gen; you went through something that was really sad and is invisible to lots of society and is misunderstood, and that's really hard.'

I think this has given me another level of understanding about the fact that we're out of control when something rubbish happens. Part of me thinks that whether you're a parent or not a parent actually it all boils down to the same things: we're human, we're in existential crisis and there is no meaning. But I don't know. At the minute I'm really trying to work on having a more self-compassionate attitude to myself where it's okay to just sit with where we are and see what happens. I do think childless women struggle with meaning and purpose. In the occupational therapy literature there's a fair amount written about the occupation of being a mother, and I've often thought I'd like to do my own studies about the occupations of non-mothers. What happens to meaning and purpose and motivation and drive then?

I think the more we talk about it the better. When I think about what would help people in this circumstance I start at the top, more in terms of policy and legislation, because we are largely absent from policy and legislation-makers' narratives. I understand that there continues to be a big focus on families and protecting women's rights and children's rights, and I think that's necessary, but we need an equivalent for the childless as well. And I think changes in policy, legislation and media representations of childless people would influence all the other things sitting underneath, justice and health for example.

There needs to be a better recognition of how the wider society can utilise the assets of this group, and support our need to be a valued part of society.

Holly,

36, Lives in New Zealand

At around 23, 24 I woke up and I just wanted babies crazily. Immediately! I wanted to have a hoard of kids. It was really weird. These days I'm thinking one would be fine.

I'm very, very happy single. A lot of the effort I put into dating now is because I want to have kids and I don't want to do it alone. I know I could; I was raised by a solo mother and she did an amazing job but I…it's extremely scary. I know a few women who've done it by themselves and boy did they rely on their mothers, and my parents are both gone. So I'd like a partner but I'm not desperate enough to shack up with anybody, and I haven't been particularly successful at dating. I fluctuate between being in a holy fuck 'I'm running out of time, what the fuck am I going to do about this situation!' (excuse my language) some of the time, and most of the time just being really happy single, putting myself out there and trying to be open to possibilities. It's very hard to find men who want to have children who don't already have them. The ones who do

– and who want a long-term relationship – are in the middle of that at the moment. I'm optimistic for my 40s and 50s, for the next wave, when the divorcees are available!

I recognise that there's a biological imperative in wanting to have children. I regularly joke that I wouldn't mind not having ovaries so I didn't feel so inclined to have kids, but I'm a vet, and I think that's vet humour! We de-sex animals all the time and it's like, 'You guys look so much more relaxed without ovaries or testes!' I love children, and I think it would be a lot of fun to have them. I always imagine that I would carry on some of the family traditions. I haven't got specific names for my possible children but in our family we all tend to be named after people who have gone before, so I always thought I'd use my mother's name if I had a girl. I'm also quite determined that if I have children they'd have my surname! That's important to me – my family, my heritage – and passing that on is pretty important, so I'd like them to be my biological children.

Just before I turned 30 I asked my doctor if I should be thinking about getting my ovarian reserve checked, and when I was 34 I asked whether I needed to freeze my eggs. Both times they were like, 'No, don't worry! No need!' But I persisted, and I got to a really great locum GP and she said, 'It's a very sensible thing to investigate.' So I did the test, and the number I got was dreadful! I got called by a nurse in the middle of work, and they told me, 'Oh yeah, you've pretty much got no eggs left.' Great! That was a trip for me because I'm from a hyper-fertile family, and I always perceived myself as being really fertile. The results can be a bit misleading, and as it turns out I'm totally responsive with harvesting. And of course the number you get has got nothing to do with how well your eggs will be fertilised and stick and stuff, but it's a bit mind blowing to me that if I had known when I was 30 that my reserve was low, I actually had some money that I could have spent and I would have had younger eggs to freeze.

Anyway, when I was advised that my ovaries were probably below average it became clear that, medically speaking, if I was going to have my own biological children I would almost certainly need to be doing IVF. It might take five to ten years for me to find someone who I love, and it will be really hard to get eggs out in five years from now. So I decided to do a cycle to freeze some of my eggs.

I'm not even slightly intimidated by the medicine of egg freezing. I guess some people find the whole process really invasive but I'm fascinated by the medicine and the science of it so it was extremely easy for me to get my head around it all, and injecting myself and the transvaginal probe procedures were no problem for me.

I was really fascinated by the process of getting them out because at first I imagined that they'd take the follicle as it was, but actually they put a 16 gauge needle in transvaginally and they suck out the inside, with the egg attached to the inside layer. Even though I was high on midazolam and fentanyl I made sure I paid attention during the procedure, but I don't really remember it much, apart from being told the numbers. I love midazolam; I've had two procedures with it and it was just a lot of fun! I've started giving it to dogs; they really like it too! There was a lovely embryologist who was counting the eggs and two nurses. I was happy, they were happy – lots of happy people. It was very pleasant and it didn't hurt, and I got 13 eggs out! I was told that 80 per cent of them would have mature eggs in them but I ended up with 12 mature ones out which is more like 95 per cent, so I consider the whole process to be a major win. I'm a bit of an overachiever and have been bragging about how I'm an overachiever about my eggs. I'm pretty stoked!

Right now my eggs are in a freezer somewhere. Well not *somewhere*: here in a facility in the city.

I don't feel particularly emotionally attached to them as cells. If I don't get to use them, I don't really mind them going into the bin. On the other hand, if they go in the bin it seems like a shame, like wasting a meal on a much larger scale! I recognise that they're extremely precious and powerful cells – with infinite, life-changing potential – and as a resource they're extremely limited, but at the same time I shed cells all over the place: every month, and from my skin and hair, and when I cough. Maybe in a year or five from now I might feel a bit different.

I spend a lot of time thinking about how I can be positive about not having babies. I probably spend a lot more time thinking about that than about if I can't have babies, because that's a scary thought to me. It would suck! I want to have kids and I'd be sad if I didn't, but at the same time there's only so much I can do about it. My feeling about life in general is that you can't plan it; life just happens at you, and what ifs aren't something I spend too much time thinking about. I can do the part about looking after my body and looking after my gametes and stuff, and I can try and date. And I'd like to think that freezing my eggs means maybe I might get a little bit of reassurance that I don't need to panic quite so much about not meeting someone, because panicking isn't helpful. I'm trying to take a 'Let go and let God' kind of approach to it all, and also to embrace the fact that there's a lot of things about my life I really freakin' like! I really focus on the freedoms I have.

Bridget,

43, *Lives in New Zealand*

In some ways, I have lived the life that my mother would have wanted to live.

She married when she was 21 and had me when she was 24. But she had a lot of stuff from her own family to sort out, and she was a reluctant mother. It would have been much better if she just hadn't married – if she'd travelled, done what she really wanted to do, met my father later on, seen a therapist, got herself sorted out.

She was quite heavily into being feminist and I went to a private girls' school. It was the 1980s, and the focus was very much about getting girls into sciences and into being professional women in the workforce. We were always told that you could have it all and I have often thought about that. No; actually, you can't. You can't have everything.

My parents separated when I was 13. My father was a doctor, and he was extremely busy doing maternity and delivering babies so he wasn't around a lot when I was young. He was very strong and I adored him. There was really virtually no emotional bond between my mother and me though. She had a really strong temper and would fly off the handle easily, and I was sensitive, so my childhood was quite traumatic. I always assumed I would get married and have children, but even as a teenager I was more interested in when I would be able to be free to have more autonomy and control over my own life, in getting through school, in surviving.

In my 20s I really felt that I needed to sort myself out. I could see aspects of my mother in me and I was determined – when I had kids – not to do what my mother had done. It's difficult to find a good therapist though, and I think part of the reason I didn't end up having children is that I was in my mid-30s before I found one that could help me.

I have often wondered about my intense need to resolve my relationship with my parents. I think it comes down to blood. It's the fact that I can't walk away from it; there is some much deeper bond there that I have to resolve. For me the parent/child relationship is a psychic bond that can be stretched but never really broken. And in not having a child I've felt the loss of being able to love someone in a really, really deep way, being able to nurture and create a space for that child to become their own person, having an ongoing continuous relationship that was always going to be there.

In my early 30s I got very run down. I left the industry I was in, and I essentially escaped to Australia. I had the idea that I would meet someone over there and create a life for myself. That didn't happen. I had three relationships but they were all quite thwarted and difficult. Australia and I didn't really mix well.

So my 30s were almost a grieving time, where I started to prepare myself for not having kids. At the same time, I just kind of got on with my life. That whole ten-year period was a difficult time, off and on.

There has always been quite a strong part of me that feels like I can't have what I want, especially around relationships and stuff like that. I know that it's from some of the old wiring from the childhood stuff: feeling like I can't really rely on anyone else, I have to look after myself. So, things like work I certainly have proved to myself that I can do almost anything that I want. But a relationship, children – those sorts of things are much more difficult. I've never felt that I'd be able to create a relationship which was stable, and where I would feel confident that I could have a child and be supported.

And I was afraid. I'm quite a pragmatic person, and having watched friends bring up kids I know it's hard work. It's tough! I didn't want to bring a child into the world on my own. I didn't want to be trying to be a parent as well as work, as well as trying to juggle financial things. I didn't want to bring a child up where I was living in a rundown old house, struggling to find money for food and having to rely on my parents for top-up things for 20 years. That's not a life, and that wasn't a life that I wanted to bring a child into. I couldn't do that.

Then at 40 I hit the wall with the having-children thing. I had just had major surgery and had a year of recuperation. I was broke, and I was back living with my parents. Up until then there had always been the possibility that I could have a child, but that birthday was a big turning point for me. It just wasn't going to happen.

I'd done a huge amount of grieving at various times, and at that point I looked at my options. I could sit and grieve. I could be an administrator, be good at my job (but not enjoy it) and slowly draw into myself and retreat. Or I could do something different. And I thought, if this is it, if I'm not going to have a child, then I'm not willing to grieve for my whole life. Yes, I'm not going to have kids, and I may not be in a relationship – I would like to be but that may not happen either – but I'm not going to sit and wallow in it.

I decided to go back to university, because I saw that if it was a matter of doing something else, then I needed to recreate a new life for myself, including my work. It was a huge challenge for me; I hadn't been in study for 20 years.

It took me a long time to decide to go into counselling. Choosing that was about coming to the realization that I wanted to work with people in more depth, and it was about being creative and nurturing. For me, that can be around creating and nurturing children, but it can also be around the creative birth and nurturing of ideas, projects and concepts. I realized I can channel my creative female energy creatively and constructively in many, many different ways. As a counsellor, I notice that I'm good at working with people in transition, but I'm not good at working with people who are grieving. And I know it's because I haven't really come to terms with my own grief and loss about children.

There are times when grieving is especially hard. Christmas and New Year. When my Mum talks a lot about family or friends and their children and grandchildren. And when I'm around lots of parents with children. It's another world: a world of preschool and school and a whole lot of networks and connections that happen as a result. Parents have a natural ease and way with children that I just don't have, because I haven't been around them.

I don't actually talk about the grieving to too many people. I don't think they really understand. I mention it every now and then to other single friends, but I don't go into any depth. I don't want to burden even close friends with my grief. I think I would cry a lot, as I have talking about it here, and I just don't want to do that. And I actually don't know how some of my other friends have come to terms with it, and to what extent they are sitting on the same sort of emotional depth about it that I am. It feels like a Pandora's Box at times.

I have made some good friends who have two boys – one's seven and one's four – and they've been great. They always talk about me being part of their family, being an aunt, and that's lovely. They're highly intelligent and lively children and I like playing with Lego with them, reading stories; it's good, it's fun. There's a kind of bittersweet quality to it sometimes, but mostly it's fine. And you know, being a mother is hard, and even just being around these friends and their boys there are days when I'm so pleased I can leave! I don't have to deal with the temper tantrums and the incessant problems and challenges of being a parent.

So there are days when my life feels definitely like a second choice. And there are days when it feels like it's actually a *good* choice.

Yvonne,

46, Lives in England

Growing up in a Caribbean household in London there were a lot of messages about the 'right' way to start a family. Getting married was the expected first step. There was this term, 'Baby Madda' – or sometimes, 'Baby Mama' – and I absolutely hated it! It was associated with women who got pregnant for a man and never became his wife, and my friends and I were adamant we were not going to become anyone's 'Baby Madda'. For me it was a derogatory term that symbolised that I wasn't good enough to be someone's wife.

In my 20s and 30s I had moments of both wanting, and not wanting, to have a child – usually depending on the relationship I was in – but I mostly didn't have a great desire to be married or to become a mum. In my early 20s, and again in my late 20s, I got pregnant. I really didn't know who I was, and I *really* didn't want to be a single mum, so I decided to terminate both of my pregnancies. Those decisions were both difficult, but I always thought that it would be okay: that one day I would be married and have children under the 'right circumstances'.

In my mid-20s a close friend died, and I was devastated. I began to question everything and I felt lost. I was searching for meaning and I looked for it in a charismatic church. I really wanted to be accepted, to be liked, to be forgiven, and the premise there was, 'Your past is your past; you're all new now.' The promise that God had forgiven me – and that my past was behind me – was very comforting, and I immersed myself in the church. I can see why people find security in that environment; it was like a family where you didn't need anyone else. But after 10 years I started to feel like I no longer belonged there, and my past feelings of shame about the terminations started to resurface. I decided to leave the church, though I faced a lot of criticism for doing so. I knew I had to understand who I was, and *like* who I was, and I knew I couldn't do that if I stayed. It was tough, but by the time I reached my mid- to late 30s – about 36, 37 – I got to a point where I was happy with who I was. I was making decisions that I could cope with, and I could look at myself in the mirror and say, 'You know what? You are okay.'

I met my husband when I was 38, and he's *lovely*. I found him very compassionate and really understanding. He just accepted me and loved me for who I was, something I'd never had before. He was the first guy I'd been with where I wasn't thinking it was going to end. I got married at 39 and our first year of marriage was really nice. We had such a laugh and I really enjoyed who we were becoming. I wanted to see what more our relationship could become, and all of a sudden I wanted to see our little ones! What would our children be like? Who would they look like?

We tried for three years. I never expected to *not* get pregnant. My cousin had a baby at 40, and I've got friends who had children in their 40s, so why not me? When it came to year two of trying it became really hard because we started arguing a lot about it. You think this is supposed to be a natural thing, and it was horrible. My husband felt like he was just being treated like a piece of meat. At around 42, 43 I was sent for fertility testing, but my GP and the consultant didn't see any urgency at all. The consultant spent most of his time asking me, 'Are you sure you're that age?' and finished up asking me why I hadn't tried sooner. At the end of all the testing – with me now at 43 going into 44 – I remember sitting in the consultant's office and him saying, 'Well you have what we call unexplained infertility. We can't find anything wrong with you or your husband, so there is no reason why you can't get pregnant. Just keep trying.' No care or sensitivity in it at all. He told me I was too old to be offered IVF on the NHS because the cut-off is 40, and referred me back to my GP.

I remember leaving that office, going home, and just crying. I knew instantly that becoming a mum wasn't going to happen and I was devastated. I was shocked at how sad I felt about it, because I'd never really known if I wanted to be a mother. It didn't make sense that it mattered so much, and I didn't understand why I was so sad. It was really tough.

Suddenly, I couldn't be around my friends anymore. Most of them had young kids. I'd go to their house and want to just leave and cry! I'd be on a train watching young families and have the urge to get off the train, because I couldn't hold back the tears. I couldn't look at women who were pregnant. I was in a spiral of grief, and I just wanted to lock myself away and cry. I found it so hard to explain to my husband what I was going through, and I shut down so much that he actually asked me if I wanted to divorce him.

I was fortunate in one way though, because I have a friend who is in her 60s who recognised that I was grieving. That didn't make sense to me at first, because I hadn't 'lost' anything. She introduced me to Jody Day – the founder of Gateway Women – and I went to a one-day workshop with Jody called 'Living without children', and then on to the longer 'Plan B Mentorship programme'. At the beginning of the programme I listened to other women's stories – some were single so never had the opportunity to try, some had had miscarriages and some had tried numerous rounds of IVF – and I sat there thinking, 'All these women really wanted their babies, I don't deserve to be here.' I was feeling a lot of shame about my terminations, and I felt like I didn't deserve to be a mum. I felt that if the other women heard my story they wouldn't want me there, but that didn't turn out to be true at all. It took a lot to open up and talk about it, but it helped me to forgive myself, and that was a huge step – a really huge step. I am in a very different place now than I was two years ago.

One of the things I've realised from it all is that the grief doesn't go away; you just find it easier to move through it and manage it. For me it depends how the grief hits me, and in those moments I might just stroke my hand for comfort and know that it's okay to feel that grief, that pain. I give myself hugs that no one can see. Sometimes I just remove myself from the situation, find a quiet space and allow myself to cry. I remind myself that it is okay to feel this way, and it will pass.

It took some time for me to realise that my grief was not just about not becoming a mum but about not having a child with my husband. I wrote a book about this experience: *Dreaming of a Life Unlived*.[1] Being a mum would have been a very different life, and who knows what it would have meant for us. It has been a difficult journey and I'm happy that through it I can make contact with women I never would have otherwise spoken to, and tell them that there is the hope that things can get better.

One of the things Jody asked us to do was write a letter to our unborn children. Here's the letter I wrote to the daughter I dreamed of:

9 August 2015
My Darling Regina

Please know that you were loved and desired and will always have a special place in my heart. You were named after your Grandad Reginald, who would have been so proud of you just

---

1   John, Y. (2017) *Dreaming of a Life Unlived*. London: Blurb.

as we, your parents, would have been. I dreamt of you so many times, crawling into your Dad's lap whilst he was studying and lying on his chest as you both slept on a hot summer's day.

You were part of my thoughts for so long that it broke my heart to know that you would never be; that I'd never get to know you or who you would have become. I wish I could have known you with your Dad, and see you share in your Grandad's memories. I wish I could have seen your smile and hold you in my arms when you cried. I wish so much for you.

You will always be in my thoughts.
Your loving Mum X

Deborah,

45, *Lives in New Zealand*

Growing up, I never doubted that I would marry and have children. That was what adulthood meant; it included parenting and being a spouse. I grew up in New Zealand but I lived in the UK for nearly ten years from my mid-20s to mid-30s. I had always imagined that I'd do undergraduate training, have some work experience, and travel and work overseas for a while. Then I would come back to New Zealand, marry and have my children and settle down – that sort of pattern.

That's not how it worked out. I went to the UK, I developed a fantastic network of friends, and I didn't think for a moment about leaving. Actually, I thought seriously about staying forever. I probably didn't even think about it; it's just that time ticked by, although I think I was conscious of the fact that I was getting older and was still single.

I had never considered having children outside a long-term relationship. It just wasn't something that I was going to do. But I work with women and children and I was only too well aware of how much my fertility was affected by my age, and that it was decreasing all the time. Rapidly. I had a sense that if I was going to form a long-term relationship that involved having children, I didn't have much time. I went back to New Zealand, met my partner, and we were living together within two years.

But by that stage I also came to a realization that a bigger concern for me was not so much that I would be infertile because of my age, but that my age increased the risk of having a child with disabilities, and I had experienced how difficult that could be. I mean there are just no guarantees. I couldn't do it.

I was fortunate because my husband didn't strongly want to have children. If we had been in this position in our mid-20s, rather than our late 30s, we might have made a different set of decisions. I suspect, reflecting back on myself, I would have been a much bigger risk taker at 25 than I would have been at 35.

But it was an incredibly difficult decision. It was difficult because I had never – and in a way still haven't – relinquished a sort of sense of myself as a mother. It's very hard to describe. I guess I've never relinquished the idea of myself as a parent, nurturer, type of person.

And it's still difficult. It continues to be hard because I would like to have been a mother. And I can't work out whether that was because I always expected to be – and for a variety of reasons I'm not – or whether it's because I value nurturing capabilities within myself. And I'd like to, I don't know...use those capabilities more? Have more opportunity to develop them, as a mother. For all my involvement in the young lives of my godchildren and my nieces and nephews, at some level I think there's a bit of me that feels like I missed out on something. That there's a life experience that I would like to have had, and I haven't had, and I'm not going to have. I would like to have had the experience of being pregnant and delivering a baby, and those sorts of things, in order to really have the experience that a lot of other women are talking about. I would just like to know it for myself.

I have a very clear picture of the children I might have had: a boy and a girl. I have given them names – Alisdair and Elinor – and I can hear their voices, just as though they are 'down the back'. That's the term we used at home when I was a child to mean playing on the farm, somewhere distant from the house but never far enough away we couldn't hear the cowbell signalling it was time to come home for a meal or some other reason. I realize that I continue to 'mother' them because I give them life in my head.

It's not loss in the sense of something known, like if you lose a parent, or a sibling – loss in the sense of having something that was known to exist and then losing it. It's not loss in that sense, and yet it is loss of…I don't know, a vision or a hope or a dream or an expectation. There is grieving that goes with it. That sense of loss and the grieving for something not fulfilled is, you know, does, exist. Yes.

I think it's been a very long process of grieving for me. Through a variety of people and relationships, and a reasonably prolonged period of quite structured personal development, every time it comes up, I look at it again. I wouldn't say I've dealt with it. I think probably, hearing the shake in my voice now, feeling the tears in my eyes, I know I will talk about it with my partner again. Talking about it brings stuff up and I think, 'Yeah, okay, I thought I dealt with that, but maybe I'm going to have a look at that again, and see how that feels, and why it provoked that reaction, where this grief – or this sense of loss, or this sense of being distressed – where's it coming from. Why does it feel that way? What's that about?'

Probably the times when it's most painful for me are when I feel someone else is making an assumption – or a judgment – about the fact that I don't have children. I remember a conversation with my brother, who does have children, over the phone. I think I was offering to do something with the children and he said to me, 'Get your own children, and don't steal mine!' And I just, I didn't say anything. I've never said anything to him about it, but it's that sort of thing that brings back the sense of 'Oh, God! It's not fair!', or 'I really wanted to have children and it's not my fault', or 'How dare you think I'm a selfish old cow!'

Those are the times, I think, when I feel the pain the most; when I feel that people have no reason to be making that judgment. Somehow there's something about me that isn't acceptable. I feel the judgment is that if I'm without children then I don't like them, I don't want to be involved with them, don't understand them, don't have experience, won't be any use.

One of the struggles I've had is that mothering would have been the obvious outlet for the nurturing parts of me, and I don't have that. And yet I still see places, relationships, roles in my work, where those parts of me exist, and are used, and are valued, and so on. It's a tension: if you're not a mother then you're not considered maternal, or you're not nurturing, or you're not something. There is an element in society in which women without children are labelled as being 'not maternal', or being 'powerful', or 'strong', or 'masculine', or various things which suggest that they're not motherly, nurturing sorts of women. And I don't think that's true. I think there are all sorts of reasons why women may not have their own children. And some of those reasons are not by choice.

Sometimes I find it painful. Sometimes it's not. Sometimes we see it is a blessing, sometimes we see the pain. And…it's not good, it's not bad; it just is.

Brigitte,

40, Lives in England

It wasn't about finding the right man because I wanted to have children. It was about finding the right man and, if it was fantastic, then thinking about having children. I couldn't seem to find the right man.

I've had four main relationships. My first was my husband. I was in my late 20s when we got married. I wasn't sure if our marriage would last and, having come from a broken home myself, I didn't want *my* children to come from a broken home. Since my divorce, I've had three relationships. One was a guy who was about 11 years older than me, and he had children. It wasn't the right time for him, and we ended up splitting up anyway. The next guy was 11 years younger than me, and I did consider having children with him but, as much as I loved him, I thought he was far too young and needed to grow up basically. Now I'm in a relationship with Aaron. He's a bit older than me – he's 46 and I'm 40 – and he's been married. He's got two kids: Amanda who's 15 and Sam who's 12.

We've only been living together as a couple for about seven months, and the kids live with us every second week. It's all very quick really, but I suppose when you get to our age you don't mess about.

I've never felt a strong sense of family because my parents split up and there were no brothers and sisters, no cousins or aunties and uncles. With Aaron for the first time in my life I've really sensed what a family is. I get on really, really well with the kids, and I feel lucky to have them. But they're not my biological children and, ultimately, as they grow up – because I've had step-parents as well – I know that you can't even compare the love that you feel for a step-parent to a parent. Because you love your mother or your father unconditionally really, they're always going to be your mum and dad. So as Amanda and Sam grow up and there's things happen – like a university degree ceremony or something like that – I'll be invited but I'll always be on the outside a wee bit.

It's good in some ways being in a relationship with someone with children. Often when you meet new people the first question is, 'Have you got kids?', and I can say, 'Yes I've got stepchildren.' And then when there's a discussion as to issues about children or teenagers and what it's like and all that sort of thing, I can add something. You've got that area of commonality that you can talk about. I noticed it just recently when I had a catch-up coffee with a friend and when I asked her about the kids it wasn't me just saying, 'How are the kids?' It was me genuinely wanting to know because now I can relate to the sort of ages that they're at and what they'll be like. She's got two boys, and I said, 'Gosh Sam's room is just so messy.' 'Oh tell me about it!' she said. 'You can't see the carpet for stuff in Lachlan's room!' and we were just laughing about it, you know. It's good to be able to relate to people in that way. I have a greater appreciation of what it's like to have children and look after them and live with them. I don't have a problem with women who choose to be childless. Some women just don't want to have children. I think it's more important that the people who want to have children have children, and if a woman has a child just because they feel they have to, then that child's not going to be loved.

I didn't choose not to have children, but as I was going through my 30s and not meeting anyone – beginning to think I wasn't going to have children – I would put up wee barriers and think about all the reasons why it was good not to have children – 'Children are just a pain in the rah, rah, rah and they cost too much money. I've got so much freedom as a woman without children' – and all that sort of thing. But there's a nugget deep down that I just tried to push down and ignore that's going, 'Well actually you do really care about having children.' I just put up this front and pretend that it's not a problem. I think I even said to my friends at one point, 'I don't think I'm going to end up having children and that's fine. I'm not just being philosophical about it.' It's a way of protecting yourself really, from all the hurt and the disappointment: the hurt from not being able to have that connection with your own child and just not having your own children. You won't have your legacy in the world or be able to watch them go out into the big wide world and have children and grow up. It's just you, and when you die there's nothing to say that you were here.

It's hard at unexpected times. Sometimes seeing a really cute kid on the street or a happy family together, and I just think, 'Oh, ow!' Or once, I was reading a book and there was a particular part that was so beautifully written about a woman who looked at her child and saw a mirror image of herself – a 'carbon copy' I think she put it – and I just thought, 'Oh gosh. That hurts.' You know?

I just bury that hurt. I tend to block things out; they get shut away in the dark deep recesses of my mind and get dragged out every so often and then very quickly put back again. Because they hurt.

It's definitely a loss. It's weird because you haven't really lost anything, because you didn't have it in the first place in a way. But there's that loss because you haven't got it; you haven't had that chance. I suppose you could describe it as grief really. Thinking of it now, I can feel the tears welling. I guess talking about it I become aware of how important it is to me.

It's not a socially accepted loss, because it's like a taboo no one talks about. I mean I don't talk about it to myself, because I don't want to go there, but I don't talk about it to other people either. I have a friend who's also childless but we don't discuss it. I don't want to probe too much for her because I sense pain there, and I don't want to upset her. Because it's grief, and there's a sense that it's a hard subject. It's like when somebody dies you say, 'I'm really sorry to hear about your loss,' but you don't tend to broach it any further than that.

If I'm with a group of people and there are lots of children running around I'm sometimes suddenly conscious that I don't have children. I feel like a bit of an anomaly: the odd one out. I used to play touch rugby in a mixed team, mainly guys, but there were some women as well. And the wives of the older guys who had families would come down on to the pitch and they'd all talk together, and it felt like the younger women, especially ones who didn't have children like me, were excluded. It's like a club I didn't have an entry ticket to – the 'Women with Children' club. They couldn't relate to me I suppose.

I haven't seen any evidence of it changing, and I don't think it will unless women start talking about it. It needs to come out and be discussed, and for women to say, 'Hey I haven't had children because…' and for their reasons to be respected as well. If they haven't had children because they wanted to pursue a career, or they didn't want to have children for whatever reason, it doesn't mean they're a witch, or evil and horrible, wicked and selfish.

It just means that they've acknowledged they don't want to have children, and have gone on and made different choices.

Georgina,

49, Lives in New Zealand

I was born in England, and my parents were English people – of another era really – living a sort of *Brideshead Revisited* upper class type of life. When I was eight they were already running out of money, so they decided to move to New Zealand. Part of their script for me as I grew up was: 'You will go back to England, and you will marry someone with a title and a house falling down around them, and that's the way it will be.' They were always very quick to remind me that I wasn't from New Zealand – 'You're not from here' – but for me the ages of 8–18 were being experienced here in New Zealand, and those are pretty formative years. I loved New Zealand, but I didn't feel like I was allowed to belong here.

Then, when I went back to England at 18, family there said, 'Well you are one of us, but you don't quite fit anymore.' That really hurt at the time. I loved both places in different ways and I felt very confused. I felt like I was tumbleweed: blowing across the landscape but never really able to put down roots.

So geography was one thread that ran through what ended up with my being childless. When it came to children, I would find myself thinking, 'But if I'm with someone *here*, will I ever get back to *there*? Am I going to be held geographical hostage by my marital status or the disintegration of it, and never actually be able to live where I want to live?'

The other thread was fear. Mum and Dad's lifestyle in England meant that from a very young age I was left behind while they went off, burning through the inheritance. I got dumped around all over the place. I was a child, eager to please and taught to do exactly what grown-ups said. Sexual abuse was an inevitable consequence of this. There was a young guy who worked for them, and they would often leave me with him when they went out during the day. I guess I was about five or so. He would come and abuse me in my own bedroom.

There were others as well. Then there was an old bloke down the road who had stepchildren who were my age. I've always worried about those other children. When I was seven he tied me up in his hay barn and raped me, oral sex, the whole thing. I remember floating away from my body and watching everything from above. When he finished he said, 'When you're old enough we'll do it again, so we can both enjoy it.' Creep. Then he did all the things that they do: threats and things to keep you quiet. For me, that event defined my childhood to 'Before Jack' and 'After Jack'. More abuse happened later at the hand of a family friend.

The thing I have learned about abuse is that it pays no heed to social strata. I think that my parents were so wrapped up in their own lives they never bothered to see signs of what might be going on in mine. I finally told my mother about it all when I was 18, and she said, 'Well if it happened with more than one person you must have been doing something to lead them on. And you always had such blue eyes that you flashed at people.' I was gobsmacked. I remember saying, 'Mum, I was seven when I was raped. I didn't know what things were, let alone how to use them!' All through my childhood she would tell me, 'If anyone ever touched you I would kill them,' but when confronted with the fact they had, she cast all the blame on me. And she used to tell me things like, 'You're so ugly. I never wanted children. You'd better not have children because I don't want to be a grandmother. I'd never look after them, and don't expect me to love them.'

So, in terms of having children, I think that mixture of geographical confusion and fear kept coming together, and one would hit the other all the time. And while I would love to have had the hollyhocks and the picket fence, and the husband and kids, that longing kept getting blown off course by one or the other influence. I was also scared I'd end up being a terrible mother because I'd be fiercely overprotective. I know that you can't protect your child from everything, but I knew I'd try. I'd be terrified for them every time they walked out the door.

It's no surprise that trust was a bit of an issue for me. In my 20s and early 30s I went through a period of magnificent but unruly love interests. I wanted domestic bliss, but I gravitated towards men there was no point in trusting, because without the need to trust I felt I couldn't be disappointed or hurt.

I thought maybe they'd keep me going while I healed internally, and then the right person would come along.

In my early 30s I got pregnant and had an abortion. It was a terribly hard decision, but circumstance was not on my side. I told myself, 'I've still got enough time to find the right person,' and I felt I was moving towards figuring out the tension between the history of abuse and the history of geography. I was optimistic about the future.

And then…time just went on. At the beginning of 2009 – when I was 41 – I started a two-year contract working in Germany for the United Nations, which has a habit of shifting people around, two years here, two years there. In one sense that was perfect for someone who felt conflicted about where home is, but it was not conducive to creating opportunities for starting a family. It was an intense contract, and I remember thinking, 'I'm really at the last window of getting pregnant and I'm single, moving to Germany and doing a job where I'm going to be head down for two years. This had better be worth it!' There were times during that job that I felt angry because it was such high pressure, and I felt like I was sacrificing that last window. I felt I had let myself down choosing career over life, and I decided that when the contract finished I would return to New Zealand, for life over career.

When I came back to New Zealand in 2011 I had a last flurry of wondering if there was going to be any chance for me to have a child, but gradually that subsided. Then I got together with – and eventually married – a friend I'd known for years. It's wonderful to be back in New Zealand, putting down roots in a place I love, with a husband I love. Our relationship has a lot of love and a lot of trust. I adore him. He is older than me and children were off the menu. With him I've just passed rather wonderfully into menopause and I've inherited ten gorgeous grandchildren under the age of ten!

So – did I think that I would be at this point in my life without a child? No. Can I understand why I did end up at this point without a child? Yes, and I still feel it is accidental because in spite of everything, being childless wasn't an outright decision I made for myself.

I've found menopause to be totally liberating. I love it, because as a childless woman it has taken the choice away, and life is now just what it is; not what it *could* be. That is a massive relief. I feel like I'm really stepping into my power as a woman because all the trauma of being a young woman and a woman of child-bearing age is behind me now. My mother died three years ago and there are aspects of her I miss a lot, but I do feel I can speak with my own voice at last. I just love this feeling as a woman that my body and my Self are really mine now, not anybody else's.

When I think what it means to be a mother, the first thing I think of is protection and love. They are the things I yearned for in my own childhood. I've always had a very strong relationship to the landscape, and turned to the natural environment and animals for comfort. Nature gives me that connection to something else: something that rewards us when we show it care and love. I definitely do 'mothering' with my animals and plants, and I do it with my business now too. I develop treatment balms and plant essences for people to use through transitions such as menopause or when they come out of cancer treatment. And I'm developing part of my business to helping at the end of life stage: products and healing work to help those left behind as well as those passing. It's all built around helping other people feel cared for and better about themselves, and using the power of Nature to do that. So although I haven't had children, my whole business and its *raison d'etre* is about care and nurture.

In shamanic practice there is the notion of the 'wounded healer'. They say that those who have been gravely wounded in their own life can go on to be powerful healers for others. Maybe my journey was brought about to equip me for what I do now. The childless mother.

Rebecca,

48, Lives in Australia

My desire to have children kind of hit me in the back end in reverse. I never really thought I had to consciously make it happen. I only got upset about it after I realised it was too late.

It's weird. It just came from nowhere, and now I feel like a completely different person than I did before the Realisation. I call it 'the Realisation'. It was Christmas last year. I'd just spent time hanging out with my family and I was feeling really shit. I was cancelling everything I'd said I'd do. I remember being in my lounge room and thinking I would Google 'childless women'. I came across the Gateway Women website and I read the first bit of Jody Day's book – where she says, 'Welcome to your tribe' – and I just started bawling, 'Oh God. That's me!' And then I spent the next few months – it was over the Christmas period so I didn't have to go to work that much – lying on the lounge room floor, looking at the ceiling, crying and eating pizza. That was the Realisation.

It was horrendous: a big shock. I don't think I realised until it hit me how awful the prospect of not having children is. It's like a lightbulb that this is the reality of the situation for me now. Prior to that maybe I'd been successfully lying to myself, or successfully avoiding it. Or just not realising. I think for an intelligent person I'm not very intelligent sometimes! Maybe I'd been a bit disassociated from my life somehow.

If I could pin it down to one thing that explains why I didn't have children it would be not meeting a guy that I felt strongly enough about to stay with. Probably the most reasonable one was Matthew, when I was 39, and in hindsight – I've got to be careful not to beat myself up about this – I should not have gone for perfection. I should have just married him and had kids, and broken up later. Lots of people seem to do that. Someone I'm really close to told me she knew on the wedding day she shouldn't really be marrying her husband, but she wanted to have kids. What ensued was a 20-year very unhappy marriage and now they have three grown-up kids who are okay, but haven't had much in the way of loving relationship role modelling. But still I feel like she's got the prize and I haven't. In some ways that was a better choice.

I am aware enough to realise that part of it is wanting what I can't have, because when I'm really looking after myself – meditating, eating properly, going to the gym, not drinking – I actually feel my life is pretty good. I'm okay, everything is okay, I'm good. And then…Matthew sort of re-entered my life a year ago and I'm still not attracted to him – dammit – and there was almost a thought of maybe we could try again. But my chances? I think the word starts with F and ends with D!

The hard thing is that it's something that must be really deeply embedded – like a natural procreation instinct that blindsides you – because…it's the feeling of not graduating as a woman. Like all these other mothers. Even the really bloody hopeless mothers seem to have this secret quality now; they're a mother. It doesn't matter how good your life is, you can never get to that.

And now it's absolutely everywhere: the whole of the world. Everywhere I go. I can't escape. Children, pregnancy, happy couples, pregnancy announcements, engagement announcements. Next year there are potentially four marriage and pregnancy announcements at work. It's going to be a tough one. I can feel an announcement coming and I kind of go, 'Oh God, it's going to hurt! I've got to try and get away from here and this situation.' I'll cross the road when I see couples coming.

Am I grieving? I wouldn't have ever recognised any of this as grief except for Jody's book about other childless women's experience of this. I wouldn't have known what was going on; I would have just thought I'm unlucky and a bit of a shitty person because I didn't know why I didn't want to be with those happy pregnant people. I would have just put it down to me being a loner; I don't really mix well with people. I wouldn't have identified the feeling.

Those feelings are becoming stronger rather than fading away. I have a feeling of my life shrinking and being more disconnected. I see people with families being more connected, with their lives getting bigger – friends, and mother's friends, and grandchildren, and extended families – and here's me trying to find a couple of childless women friends. I'm trying to hang out with people that don't trigger pain, which is probably not the path to healing. You can't avoid it, can you?

And hearing myself now, it's all sounding really pathetic! I'd really like to reiterate that when I'm looking after myself I can overcome all that! But I feel like I'm really having to upkeep all that stuff quite strongly now to keep myself feeling okay, and I almost wonder whether these awful bloody things are sent to push us in that direction. I can't go on feeling like this; I'm going to have to rectify it somehow.

You can't talk to other people about this stuff because they don't have a clue. They don't understand. And I've noticed a strange phenomenon – maybe it's human nature when someone is a little bit down and separated from the herd – where people suddenly tell you nice stories about what's going on in their life, like my cousin who has two children. Probably I feel most envy around her; even though her husband can be mean and I do not aspire to her relationship, her children are lovely and she's doing a really great job. She has a nice relationship with her daughter who is about 14 and she was telling me yesterday her daughter calls her Mummy Bunny. Do I want to hear that? I probably don't. Sometimes it seems that the people who know of my situation (and there aren't many of them) can tend to put in subtle comments and it feels as if they are designed to poke my pain, to trigger some response. What are those comments designed to do? I don't understand; they know my situation. So I don't talk about it anymore. Not that I ever did extensively, apart from the initial announcement to a select few after the Realisation.

But I've missed all of that: the whole plaiting someone's hair, buying them little clothes, sending them off to school, watching what choices they make, having them say, 'Mummy how do I cut this carrot?', watching them get married, having children, everything. It's everything actually. I can't believe I didn't realise; what was I doing? I feel like I've been dreaming. I just can't believe it sometimes. I wake up and go, 'Oh my God! I can't believe this is my life!'

Meditation definitely helps me, though I've fallen off the gym and meditation wagon for a few weeks. I do notice a subtle profound difference when I'm doing it. It makes me feel more even. Probably only ten minutes a day makes a difference for me. Also alcohol is a big thing as I get older; I notice a negative slide in my attitude and thoughts about everything in general when I am drinking even as little as one or two glasses of wine every other night, so more and more I am having longer and longer spells of not drinking at all. Alas, alcohol is not my friend anymore.

I've had quite a lot of recovery and I've even been good in the times that I've been looking after myself. So I think possibly I'm healing quite well but I've got to move through some of this anger, because I can't do that for the rest of my life. I think the anger is with myself, and with the powers that seem to make it possible for it to happen for almost anyone else at any age, but not me.

I describe myself at the moment as childless, but I have this fantasy that I need to get myself to an emotional place where I could describe myself as childfree. I'm not sure how I'm going to do that yet, but I'm not doing the rest of my life as childless. I'm not doing that. I'm going to have to learn something to move through it. To live the next 50 years missing something? No.

Rachael,

46, Lives in New Zealand

I work as an artist – primarily a painter – and in marketing, and I've worked my way into management up to CEO level. People have looked to that as being an excuse for me not having children; I've had both women and men say, 'Oh, you've focused on your career,' but I correct them. Actually my success has been a default of the fact that I haven't had the opportunity to have children. I would have rather had a family any day; I'd give all this up in a heartbeat for that.

Having a family wasn't ever a question for me. It wasn't even a decision; it was intrinsic, an absolute presumption that that would be part of my life. But my parents had a very acrimonious divorce when I was younger that was really tough on us children, so probably more than most people I was very aware of the fallout from divorce. I was adamant that if I brought children into this world I wanted to create a really strong foundation for them, surrounded by unconditional love. Those were the circumstances that I needed to do it, and I just didn't meet the right person to do it with.

As time started running out in my mid- to late 30s I got involved with someone who had prior family. He paid lip service to the idea of having children with me, but he didn't really commit to it. That's one thing I've chosen to flag with women; figure that out early on because sometimes you get led onto it being a possibility when it's not, and then when you realise, you're like, 'Wow! Well there goes three years.' I wasted serious time with him.

When I was 38 I heard that egg freezing had recently become available privately in New Zealand if you fronted up with $10,000, and I thought it was the most constructive thing I could do. I was one of the first here to do it. I did one round and they recommended I do another one, but that was another $10,000 I didn't have at the time. In hindsight I wish I'd done more; I tried really hard to keep my body in the best shape I could for potential pregnancy and at one stage it would have been $1500 to $2000 a month on acupuncture, vitamins, treatments, you name it. I got five eggs out, and I thought, 'Well there's my little insurance policy.' I knew it wasn't a great one. Ironically, I was still really convinced I wouldn't need it.

It was hard trying to fit the preparation for the egg freezing process into my normal life. I was working between two cities at the time, and I'd have to fly with my little kit of injections. I'd land, get off the plane and go to the toilet to inject myself. I was literally shooting up in the airport! God, who'd have thought I'd be doing that.

My Mum was my support person for the retrieval procedure, and when I actually had the eggs taken and they passed the first vial to the embryologist, she said she saw this little spark of light as it went across the room. So she bought me a necklace with a Swarovski crystal in it, and she said, 'That's your seed; that's the life that's going to get created.' That resonated for me; I'm a fifth generation New Zealander, and family – that sense of *whakapapa*[1] – is really important to us. We have things that have been passed down five generations.

As time continued to go by with no one in sight to have a child with I became more distressed. The real kicker was that I'd actually got to the stage where financially I could do it by myself. Before that I just couldn't figure out how to make it work financially. It wasn't until I felt I had enough income and I'd managed to get a house and all those things that I thought I could probably afford to have a baby. But of course by the time I achieved that I was in my early 40s, and that was almost diametrically opposed to timing for having a child.

Then a very credible friend – who was trying to get pregnant at the time herself – told me that she believed I could give children a better platform than a lot of children coming into this world, and for the first time, I considered doing it alone. I spoke to my brother first. I told him that I was thinking of having a child on my own and I said, 'If I do this, do you think you might be a bit of a special uncle?' I think children need men in their lives. Good men.

I really struggled with the whole donor sperm thing. I had some unsuccessful attempts to find someone, and then

---

1   A Māori word meaning geneology, the family line traced back to one's ancestors.

I had a very chance conversation with somebody who said, 'Yeah I'll help you.' It felt right, but it was a long process. He'd had a vasectomy when he was a lot younger so he needed to have an operation to do sperm retrieval, then there had to be a cooling-off period for three months, and then he had to go through counselling. I was so, so excited by that stage. It was certainly not an ideal scenario, but it was a pretty good scenario, and I went into that transfer feeling great about it.

First they thawed the eggs, and this was back when this technology was all pretty new and experimental. Five out of five eggs thawed – which was great! – but then they didn't fertilise. It got to the stage where they called me and said I wasn't going to get any at all. I was heartbroken. The next day they called again and said, 'We've got one embryo.' The transfer was really good, and I just did everything they suggested for the next ten days. Then the blood test came to say that I had pregnancy hormones in my bloodstream, but they weren't increasing. That meant I had a biochemical pregnancy, where initially it had taken, and then it didn't. I felt a really great sense of loss when they didn't fertilise, but I felt the greatest sense of loss about the embryo. I guess you reconcile the loss of the eggs a little by the fact that you already lose eggs each month, but when that egg become fertilised it became a whole other scenario.

By that stage I was so excited about having a family and my dream coming true, I just wanted to do another cycle. They told me my chances were very low at my age and I said, 'I don't care.' We planned three back-to-back cycles of IVF again to try and bank more – maybe one or two eggs a time – and I was like, 'Let's just see what we can get.' That was in February this year and I haven't had a period since. So for some reason – in the worst possible timing known to man – it looks like I might have gone into early menopause. At the moment I have blood tests every two weeks to see if my hormone levels have changed at all, but it's not looking good.

It's funny; you have all these boundaries, and they just keep shifting as you go along this journey. At first I found the idea of using a sperm donor too hard, and then I got my head around that, but was absolutely sure I couldn't use an egg donor. I thought if they can't be mine biologically then maybe – maybe – this is the end of the road. But I just couldn't face that to be honest. So what I've done in the interim – while I'm still hoping and praying and drinking fertility tea – is that I heard about a girl who had made this really flippant comment that she'd help. I put the feelers out on that and it was another 'What if?'…but another dead end.

I imagined a boy and a girl. I have names for them, and some clothes and toys. I tried not to get too carried away, but my Mum knitted some booties that I always keep with me, and I have that necklace she bought for me – things that are symbolic to me about that dream. That imagined family has been such a big missing part of my life. I've had wonderful experiences, but there's this gaping hole that you could drive a truck through. Nothing has really compensated for that.

In an interesting twist of fate I have met someone who already has a daughter, and this has further triggered my maternal instinct. We want to have children together, but my body is not responding. So another chapter begins in terms of how we might make that happen. It's not over. I am going to have a modern family!

Teena,

47, *Lives in New Zealand*

A lot of people have said to me, 'You'd be a great mum, you're very good with children,' but I don't see myself like that. And if I'm to be honest a big part of why I didn't have children is that I didn't have the best relationship with my own mother. I just never had a great bonding experience with her. She went through a heavy drinking stage when I was about 11, and when I was 14 she and Dad separated, which was the best thing ever, because they were just not getting along at all. They were still each other's best friends afterwards, and neither of them ever re-married. But I left home after they separated and went to live with my sister, because I didn't want to be living alone with Mum.

It's not that I didn't feel loved with her, because I did, but I guess…it was a bit dysfunctional at home. When I got older and more independent – and as she got a bit more mellow with age – my relationship with her did improve. But that's always been in the back of my mind. I'm not sure that I would have

– I'd like to think I wouldn't – but if I had a child I'd just hate for that relationship to be the same – to pass that on. Because it's not uncommon for women to have children and then go through post-natal depression. If I had that, and then I never felt a bonding with my child…I would just be really frightened that that could happen. So that's always been there.

I regretted leaving home later, because Dad then went back into the house after the separation. With Dad it was different; we've always gotten along a lot better and I had a close relationship with him. I can talk to him about anything, and I would have lived at home if he had stayed there. And who knows what would have happened then? But by the time he moved back I'd left school and started working. Leaving home and having to get a job because I wasn't going to stay with my sister forever – that sort of helped to drive my independence, and it was probably responsible for the most part for the life I've ended up with. I mean I would have left home anyway, but I'm not sure that I would have become so independent in the way I am. That was a big part of why my partner and I haven't married as well; because we don't have children, we never felt the need to and we don't see it as being an important thing. I guess I've sort of been able to remain independent in every way. I have travelled quite a lot without my partner and I like being able to just go, just not having any strings attached.

I met him when I was 18 and we've been together ever since. The age difference between us is quite substantial: 17 years. We moved into a council flat first for six months or so, then we moved into a two-storey hotel in the city and lived upstairs.

My partner was bar manager there, and I had a full-time career. I started as an office junior at 17 then moved up. After three years in the hotel we got our own first home: an old rented farmhouse in a beautiful location at the top of a valley in a rural/city location. We lived there for eight years and to the day we left the owners had never finished decorating it. The walls were stripped and stopped, and that was it. It was a lovely place, lovely setting, very idyllic.

That was really when we first talked about having children, after we'd been living there a year or so. It was always just a conversation at that stage. I would have been about 21 and we both agreed that it wasn't the right time, and we weren't in the best place to have children, so a 'not right now' kind of thing. In the eight years we lived there I had a few job changes – advancing my career along the way – and then we left and bought a house here in the Bay when I was 29. Our house is on a hill, two storeys, but just garage underneath. It's not a place that you'd do up; it's just too old and would require too much work and money thrown into it. We kind of saw the place as somewhere we'd just spend a bit of money on – make it more comfortable – but not really the kind of place you'd raise a family. We talked a bit more about children after we bought the place, and we decided that the Bay would be a great place to raise a family but not in that house. At that point, having children was not off the table, that's for sure.

We'd been living there about six years when I got my current job. I would have been 33, and during that time from when we arrived and talked about it we just...I don't know, the time went really quick, we were just loving the change of lifestyle and living here. And there was always a bit of a financial pressure. I've always been fortunate and earned good money but my partner has never really been able to earn good money with the sort of jobs he's done, and he hasn't worked full time for quite some time.

We did talk about having children again, obviously. When I was 26 or so I went through this period where suddenly I really had this strong desire to have children and I thought, 'Hmmm this is going to be interesting,' – because it really wasn't a good time to do it – 'perhaps it will go away,' and sure enough in six months it did! I never had that desire again. I've never really… it's never really bothered me. When we did have the talk my partner was open to it; he was like, 'Whatever you want. If you want to all good, if you don't, that's fine too.' He was fine either way, which surprised me, because I really thought he would want to have children. He's great with kids; kids love him and he loves kids. It just was all too easy and I thought, 'Gosh, I don't really have to do this.' I do feel bad to some extent about it; I mean we came to a mutual agreement but he hasn't had that opportunity and he would be such a good father. And if it weren't for my own personal feelings because of my early home experience then maybe I would have considered it more. But I'm happy with how things are.

So I guess as far as the house went, and my career, plus the finance factor – one thing and another the time has really gone quickly. We're both quite selfish too; we like our lifestyle here and we love our animals. We've got a dog and cats, and we get a lot of love out of them. And in a year's time my partner will be getting superannuation. It's funny how it's all worked out really.

We talked a lot about having a sense of purpose in your life if you don't have children. We came to the conclusion that a lot of people believe that it's the right thing to do – what's expected – and that's what you do. People have children for selfish reasons too; they just want to see what their offspring is going to come out like. But at the same time we both think we've been selfish in our decision not to. We'd have to change so much about our life and lifestyle...

Sometimes I do wonder – I guess because most of my friends and family and everyone has got children – if I'm going to be lonely and on my own in 20 or 30 years. My father is 81 now, my partner is a lot older than me, and my siblings are all quite a bit older than me too. So I do think I could be a lonely old woman one day. I mean that's probably my main regret – which is again very selfish – that's what I think about the most, besides the obvious things like not being able to share my life and experience with offspring. Staying independent, and not being dependent on someone or having someone dependent on me, is important to me. I get scared about getting older because I may not have that independence that I would like to have. I may not have anybody to rely on.

But that's my decision. My partner and I have talked a lot about that possibility as well. And you know, you could spend all that time nurturing kids and doing everything right, and then they could just turn against you anyway, or go overseas.

There are no guarantees that they are going to be there for you later in life, or that you will have a good relationship with them. That would just be the worst thing.

Rose,

41, *Lives in New Zealand*

I always thought I'd be a mother, always. I always thought I'd be married. I used to play with a piece of lace and I'd pretend I was a bride with a long lacy train. And I always wanted babies. But I never really connected with anyone long term; the longest I've had was 11 months when I was 20.

I think about it a lot, and I wonder why. I don't know whether it's to do with my relationship with my father and brother, and experiences I had with men as a child. I think I was sexualised early and in my late teens and early 20s I was quite promiscuous. That affected my ability to connect with men on another level other than just sexual. I guess I just don't know what to do with men.

Five years or so ago I was quite distraught about not having had a child. My parents influence me a lot, and my Mum spent a long time going on and on and on: why am I not with someone, all these other people seem to manage it and why can't you? And she wanted grandchildren; all her friends had grandchildren…that kind of stuff. But now I'm actually reasonably comfortable with things, and the biggest thing in that change is the influence of my parents. I think they've gotten used to the fact that it's not going to happen. I have one sibling – a brother – but he's 46, and he doesn't want children. So the family genes stop with me and my brother.

I still hold onto a little bit of hope. I still have my monthly cycle, so I'm not going through menopause yet. But I'm on another path now – nursing – that I started four and a half years ago, and I think that has in some way filled the gap.

I was attracted to nursing because I want to be able to care for people. I don't have anyone to care for. My parents won't let me care for them; they're too staunch, and even though they need a bit of support, they refuse. So I guess it's about finding an opportunity to find my caring side and utilise that part of my personality that I don't get to use. And also I was drawn to it because nursing is a respected role or position in the community, and I just felt I had more to offer than fixing the photocopier in an admin job. I've done pretty well; I got top student award, and now I just have to live up to that on the job, which is a wee bit daunting. There's a lot to learn.

I did consider having a child on my own. My contract to myself was that if I didn't have a child at 35 I'd do it myself, but then when I got to 35 I could see friends that have done things on their own and I just couldn't fathom that: financially being able to look after a child. I don't think it's fair on the child really, to go through all that stress, because they would pick up on the stress and anxiety. And I also didn't think my parents would approve, and my parents' approval has always been quite important. I didn't want anyone to feel obligated to support me.

So I got to 35 and thought, 'Oh maybe 40,' but the older I've got, the less strong my feelings towards having children have been. I know some women are very strongly maternal and go through a huge mourning period when they come to that decision but I don't think that's really happened for me. Maybe it's because I'm a huge procrastinator anyway, and I kept thinking, 'Oh there's always tomorrow. Maybe something will happen.' I have moments where I feel very maternal and want to go out and hold all the children and have snuggles, and there's other times when they start screaming that really ear-piercing scream, and I think, 'Oh thank goodness for that!'

I think the time of feeling distraught around my mid-30s led me to the decision to go nursing. I wondered what I could do: what I could fill my life with if I don't have children. It was more about looking forward to where I'm going to be at 50 and 60. It was more about the sense of being alone, as opposed to not having children: the thought of not having anyone to watch out for me and look after me when I'm older. At the moment I've got my parents but in ten years' time they won't be here.

I do get sad when I look at other people and their wee children, wondering what it's like to feel that connection with them. What it's like to have that unbreakable bond and that really strong love that they talk about. I wouldn't know what that feels like, and I'll never experience it. I always thought it would be interesting to be pregnant and see what that felt like, and breast-feeding and all of that. My body has sort of gone to waste a bit really, because it hasn't done what it was meant to do.

I do worry that once I absolutely can't have children I'll feel a sense of regret. At this stage I don't, but I think that's because I'm in a different place just at the moment in terms of the new career and everything. And at the moment I can't imagine myself being with a man long term; I've been alone so long! I haven't dated for ten years and the thought of dating and having to compromise…I don't know. It does get lonely being on my own. I go out a lot; I don't spend much time at home really. I like to be out around people, but I don't think I could live with anyone.

I tend to have depression and anxiety but I'm feeling quite stable just at the moment. I think I'm in a good place; I'm starting a new job, I've started getting back on top of my health with healthy eating and I've bought a bike. So I think I'm in a positive upwards move at the moment: in a good space. It may just be a blip, though. It just depends.

Shanti,

46, *Lives in England*

In my late teens I had a very, very strong dream about being in the middle of giving birth and going, 'I can't do this. I can't go forward or back, and I'm completely stuck.' I remember waking up and being drenched in sweat. My body felt like I had gone through what I imagined giving birth would be like. It was such a powerful dream that it's stayed with me ever since.

I was born in Wales, and when I was six months old my mother took me to New Zealand. I was raised there, without any contact with my father, but knowing who he was. My mother's relationship with him had been brief, and she was very frank about him to me: 'This is his name, he's an architect, he's in London and when you're older it's up to you to get in touch.' So I grew up thinking that if I had a child it wouldn't really matter if I was with someone or not, but it might be more practical if I was. I didn't see the use for fathers to be honest, because I'd visit friends and the mums would always be welcoming, but the dads usually wouldn't really engage with me.

So my mother brought us up. She is a fiercely independent woman who had never wanted to get married but had wanted to have children, and she chose to have me and my sister. We lived as part of a hippy network, with a lot of amazing women and men around, and my idea of family was quite broad. She was a sex worker, and she always presented a totally rosy idea of sex and relationships. We had such a sex positive upbringing that we had no guard against the sex negative – the psychosexual damage that can happen – and the world is really sex negative. When I challenged her about that my mother would say, 'Well I never had a bad experience, so I can't really teach you about that,' but I argued that she was in a working environment where the majority of the people she worked with were really damaged, so that didn't cut it for me. I felt that as a role model and particularly as someone choosing to do something that had such an impact – even though it was never at home – it was her job to give my sister and me some skills, a more balanced reality, especially as she was so open about it. I can appreciate that openness now as an adult, but as a younger person I couldn't, and in my late teens and early 20s I was quite angry with her.

When I was 19 I wrote to my father in England, and decided to go over and meet him. He hadn't told his family about me; he'd married and I think it was easier for him just to pretend that I maybe wasn't his. I look just like him, but soon after I turned up I was asked to have a DNA test and that was really shocking for me. It was very hurtful because it never occurred to me that I wasn't his child and there was no reason for my mother to lie. I felt very angry that he questioned my mother's honesty.

A couple of years later, in London, I had the opportunity for us all to meet together for the first time. My father was quite eccentric and bohemian in his own way, but he and my mother were very different people and had different ways of responding to the situation. We met in a pub and at first they weren't really talking. I got irritated with them and went to get us drinks, and when I came back I said to my mother, 'Even though we've had some difficult times, I love you. You've brought me up really well despite our differences, and I really thank you for that.' And I said to my father, 'I'm really glad that you are you and not some straight, uninteresting person,' – because he was quite unusual – 'and I'm really glad that I met you and that you're my father and not someone else. But I'm really pissed off at you both, for not dealing with the fact that there's things that you should have dealt with about me, when I was a baby. We've all slept with someone who we didn't want to have a cup of tea with in our life, let alone a child; but I was conceived and neither of you dealt with that in a way that was helpful to me. I shouldn't have to be having a DNA test at 21, to sort out your lack of communication.'

That experience had a huge impact on my thinking about how to make a choice around having a child, and affected how I felt about having children at all. Prior to that it was very open; anything seemed possible. I'd thought if I wanted to have a child I could just get pregnant, but the DNA test totally changed my viewpoint on that. I realised that if you choose to have a child on your own no matter what choice you make about how you do that – especially if it's a choice that doesn't include the other parent – that child will grow up to have some pretty strong questions, and I became very, very aware of the responsibility for having the answers to them. I really took on board how complex it would be later on. I would be making a choice that had such huge implications for this being, and how dare I do that with such confidence and such arrogance, when actually it's really to serve myself, rather than him or her.

At that point I began to see it from my position as the child and anticipate that I might be putting another child in that position. It was very clear: I don't ever want to have to make that choice, and I don't want to have children under those circumstances. And I couldn't conceive of a relationship that would support having a child then. Two years earlier, the man who was the love of my life at that point had died in an accident, and my romantic idea of being with someone and finding the person that you would create that kind of security with wasn't there. I spent most of my 20s in no relationships at all, because I was sad, and scared, and grieving.

Then when I was 28 I met a woman and fell completely in love with her. Suddenly I thought, 'Oh my God! Does this mean I won't have children?' I had a very small but significant time of just adjusting, embracing this new sexuality, and also having a little sadness about the possibility that I might not have children. It sounds weird to say that from today's perspective, where it seems now every gay couple is having a child – I mean really, the amount of lesbians I know that are breeding is extraordinary – but at that time it was different. After a bit I let go of worrying about that as an idea because I was only 28 or so; I didn't need to think about it then. And I didn't think about it again for a long time, except for about once every year or two. People would ask me how I felt about having children, and I'd say, 'Well I've never wanted to have a child for more than a few minutes a few times a year, so that's a pretty good indication that I'm not going to miss it.'

It's really interesting as my younger queer lesbian friends start to have babies, which is happening a lot. I'm happy for them but I also find it curious, and I'm always excited by queer family structures. I think that what is interesting about them is that they are so discussed. You have to fight so hard about what marriage and a family means in a queer relationship. You can't just go and get knocked up! So I get quite excited and happy for more queer families because I think it can only be an expansive thing ultimately.

I have often questioned in a kind of devil's advocate way when people say they really want to have a baby. I will say, 'Do you want to have a baby, or do you want to parent?' because to me those are very distinctive and different things. Those are the choices that I feel people should be considering when they want to parent, and to some extent maybe that it doesn't need to be your own birth child. I've never felt a desire to parent but as I've got older I think I might be in a state now where I would. I used to think I probably didn't have the patience, and I thought I'd be a pretty awful parent, but now I realise I could actually be okay, if I have chosen to do that. At this point, having had a relationship and an open marriage with a trans man – I'm not too hung up on the gender of the person I'm with – it's about meeting the right person, and if that person has children then I just hope like hell I get on with them, and we will find our way through. Meanwhile, I love being an aunt!

Ultimately I would say I'm voluntarily childless, because I've never had to wrestle with it, but I think there are circumstantial aspects. It wasn't so much of an active choice of me saying, 'I don't want this,' but threads and experience that have woven into that being the outcome. And it's an outcome that I'm very comfortable with.

Shelley,

50, Lives in New Zealand

Looking back, what I say now is I wish I'd got pregnant when I was 18. I grew up at a time when my mother was...well, a bit moralistic I suppose, and she had four daughters. I think she lived in fear that one of us was going to get pregnant, and she did really well because none of us did.

I definitely see myself as child*less*, rather than childfree, but I've been really lucky. I never got obsessed with my childlessness. I went through the agonies of fertility treatment, and I went through the agony of having a period every month and was devastated every time it happened. But I managed to somehow keep my sanity.

I'm married now, but I think that both of the long-term relationships that I had in my life – before I met my husband – ended because of infertility. I was with Tim, the second guy, for eight years. We were trying to get pregnant and it just wasn't happening. He wanted his own biological children, so even though we talked about adoption, he wouldn't engage.

We'd had problems. He had some personal issues that caused a major depression and I'd stuck by him, but I knew things were falling apart. In the end, the day that we broke up we'd just got back from holiday. My period was late and I was just quietly going crazy – because I lived on hope, for years – and then it came. I was just devastated. He just looked at me, and said, 'Phhh, that's it. We're over.' He couldn't handle my grief and he just didn't want to be there anymore.

Part of the problem was that I had endometriosis, diagnosed in my 20s. When I was 44, 45 I saw a specialist that I hadn't met before, hoping I could have some more surgery to make it possible for me to have a child. He was very blunt. He said, 'Oh there's no point, your endometrium would be stuffed and your eggs are too old anyway so you may as well just give up!' I walked out of there *absolutely* devastated. I couldn't even go back to work. He had no idea what he'd done to me. No idea at all! That probably was the start of the end for Tim and me as well, because he just couldn't understand my grief. And it *was* grief; it was huge. It was absolutely awful.

Around that time, I spent lots of time with some really close friends and they're the ones who sowed the seed in my mind of going down the adoption path as a single woman. I thought my way through it and decided that I *could* do it actually. In March of the following year I started.

The process is huge. They run a series of full-day seminars, but before you get to that you have to go through interviews with social workers. I got particularly hard interviews because I was on my own and they had to be sure that I was doing it for the right reasons. Which was fine; I mean I *fully* appreciated that. I made the call that no single mother in the local pool of adopting mothers was going to choose a single mother for her baby – especially not one who was 45 – so I decided to go international, and after quite a lot of research and talking to people I decided to go to China. There's a whole series of meetings – it's quite intense – and then you're assigned another social worker who comes to your house and does a home report.

Your whole life is basically on the table. It was *hugely* challenging because the social worker's job was to make sure that I was 200 per cent sure about what I was doing. To adopt from China I also had to get a letter signed by my lawyer saying I wasn't a lesbian. I'm not kidding! He's actually an old school friend, and he doesn't know whether I'm a lesbian or not, but he signed it for me.

When you're allocated a child you get a letter, and with it is a picture of *your* child, all in Chinese, but you get it translated when it comes. It tells you the story of the child and where they were found. You get information about what the child eats and what they like to play with. Then you have to get permits to go to China. You go with a group of other adopting parents. You're looked after when you get there by a translator and a guide. You get to meet the children, and then the next day you're basically given the child. The day after that they take you to Beijing to do the actual adoptions and then you get the child their passport and you can bring them straight home.

But I never got that far. When your very extensive

paperwork lands in China it goes through this very long process. There's a website that you can go on to track where the paperwork is at. It took me *ages* to even try to understand it because it's Chinese translated into English by Chinese people. The paperwork was sent, and then you just wait. I waited and waited. All that paperwork has to be renewed every two years, and things kept dragging on until I was getting close to the first two-year deadline.

The turning point was a funny one. I was in Australia doing some work and I caught up with a friend of mine. He's like a little brother; we've been best buddies for years. He's a gym instructor and he said to me, 'Oh God, Shelley, my energy levels just aren't what they used to be!' He's younger than me, and it started me thinking, 'If I'm going to be a mum for the first time with a three- or four-year-old – because I would have got an older child – and he's really fit and healthy, and I'm pretty active but I'm not *that* fit, how the hell am I going to cope?' My social worker had kept in touch all through this long waiting period and when we talked it through she said, 'And have you factored menopause into that, Shelley?' It just hadn't even come into my mind.

And so…in the end, it was about being pragmatic. That really was the catalyst. I said, 'Look, how about we do it this way. When my paperwork runs out, then I'll know.' And she rang me about six weeks later and just said, 'It's happened.' The papers had come back, and I decided to withdraw the application.

I imagined that little girl a lot. I gave her a name, and

that was my biggest mistake. I called her Sophie and she was human. She was real. And that made the decision to withdraw so much harder.

It *still* makes me feel really sad. It was very tough, but I did the right thing. You think you're over it but something will happen...like, we went to this movie, at the end of last year. I can't remember what the movie was called but Colin Firth was in it. It was about a woman and right at the end – you didn't know it was coming – she adopted a little girl from China. And next thing, the end shot was her with this little girl, a huge shot right in your face. All you could see was this little girl. I just completely lost it in the movie theatre, and it was like, 'Get me out of here, get me out of here!' I had to go to the bathroom, and it took quite some time, getting myself composed again.

I've missed out on being a mum and it's a gap. It *is* a gap, in my life. There's this...thing...that you could be, and you haven't. But I will go to my grave knowing that I tried. If I hadn't tried, then I think I'd go to my grave a sad old lady, and I *won't* go to my grave a sad old lady. I'll go to my grave knowing that, you know, there could have been someone but it just didn't happen. It was sadly outside of my control, because there's nothing I could do about it because I'm not...someone like Angelina Jolie or Brad Pitt. The thing that *pisses* me off is when I read about people like that who can just do it because they have money. They can just go and do it, and all of us have to go through a process. That is not fair.

The other part of my story is that I met my husband!

He's got five adult sons and four grandchildren. So, I'm really lucky because the consolation prize is that I do still have children in my life. I still get to have little people around. I don't get to be the mother because his sons are all grown up and they don't *need* another mother, but the kids call me 'Nana'. The first time it happened I didn't feel I could step into that. They already have a Nana. But an older, wiser person said, 'Shelley, just let them call you what they want to call you. You're with their Grandad so, by their logic, you're Nana.' And I thought, 'Oh! Okay!'

Kathryn,

45, Lives in New Zealand

We tried to conceive…I think for maybe eight or nine, ten years – a *long* time. It came to a point where we went through an IVF treatment and I got pregnant for the first time. I was so excited! I knew her name, we booked a midwife, I told my boss and we told other people, I knew when I was going to finish work; I was so convinced that it was happening! And then we lost the child – quite early, seven or eight weeks – and we were devastated. I know many women go through much worse experiences than that, so it wasn't particularly special in any way, but for me it just felt like, 'Wow, this is really low.' It hit me hard. I was so incredibly exhausted by the loss and by the years of relentlessly trying and failing to have a baby. This was not how my life was meant to be.

A shift happened for me then. I was 42, and in that grief, in that moment, I got to a place where I realised something needed to change, that there was more to life than this. I spoke to a really amazing woman – a spiritual coach – and that helped me a lot. The big thing that I needed to reconcile was the loss of the dream, the movie of my life, the plan I had in my head about how life was going to be. It's like I had to re-programme. I had to decide that having children is not the only way to be happy. That was hard because all my life I wanted to have children, always believed that I would. There was never an alternative presented to me. I didn't know women who didn't have children, but of course now I know lots and they have amazing and fulfilling lives.

I started to look at things differently and even though there was a grieving process, the change happened quite quickly. It felt like once I'd made that decision to move on, things became different. The thing I remember quite distinctly is that little things became meaningful, so that all of a sudden I felt like life became exciting again and that had been lost for years. I had space for things other than trying to conceive. It's like I finally took my life off pause.

I'm from a large Catholic family – there are seven children in my family and many cousins on both sides – and I remember telling people I was going to have a large family; it was a big thing for me. I don't know what happened to stop that from becoming how my life turned out. When I was younger I was diagnosed with endometriosis and had some surgery for that. Later, I went on a quest to become as healthy as I could. For a long time, I thought if I was able to get physically well and in tune, I'd get pregnant. I had this belief it would happen and it took me a long time to realise when it wasn't happening. For a long time I played it down; I guess I wasted time looking back.

Then in my late 30s I ramped it up and got very strategic. I was in great shape and I did everything physically possible to increase our chances of conceiving. That's when it became so controlling; you're taking your temperature, you're taking pills and supplements, you're timing when intercourse happens, and everything is very controlled and of course, all consuming.

And that's when the joy got lost. That happened for years. I went from one thing to the next thing, I want to try this, and try this, and we'll try this technique, and let's look at our relationship, and I'll leave work and have some time off...our whole life was based around conceiving. I knew it wasn't okay, but the whole time I felt like I had to maintain this front that it was and that I was coping.

For me the change that made the difference was a process of letting go – letting go of the life I thought I would have, the plan, the dream of being a mother, of having a family. It was a journey – I used to hate that word, but it's the only way I can describe it – in physical ways, emotional ways, in my relationships, and then a spiritual one in the end. I'd already done some training in meditation way before the IVF and miscarriage and so that definitely helped me prepare to let go. It gave me a tool and a way to understand the concept of accepting what is. I know now that life isn't always what you think it's going to be. Letting go of that dream is the hardest thing I have ever done.

And after that 'journey' I don't feel a sense of sadness about my experience. I feel like...it sounds a bit dramatic but almost an awakening or a new beginning – a new opportunity.

Like a shedding. I feel like the vision I had of my life, of being a mother and wife and having this family, was perhaps restrictive, and there's been a huge learning of trust to accept that maybe that wasn't meant to be. Whether it was or wasn't, I don't know, but this is where I am. Maybe there's something more for me. It's led me to a better place than before I started trying to get pregnant. I feel like I'm a much more open person. I'm stronger, I'm wiser and I trust life way more.

Even when the decision was made to let go though, there were still layers of grief to work through. I think the only thing that still makes me sad – I can feel it now, talking about it – is for my husband, because I still feel like I wasn't able to give him children. I know it makes him sad and he hasn't quite let go, and I feel sad because I can't control that.

So I've come eventually to a place of peace and acceptance about my life and my childlessness. And from that place I thought that maybe I could share my experience and what I have learnt with others. A big part of my experience was that people didn't really understand. It was a really difficult thing to talk about, and then on top of that people just didn't really get it. I spent most of my time feeling alone and isolated. I didn't know how to talk about what I was going through. So from that was born a one-to-one coaching service: Fertility Potentials. I'd coached before but not specifically with women who were going through infertility. It's about providing something that I really needed on my journey; I don't want anyone else to feel as alone and overwhelmed, and all the other emotions that come with infertility, as I did. I want to provide a space that's safe, supportive and understanding for women to come and share their experiences, and that eases a lot of that grief and burden. There's no judgment, no trying to fix it or them. I guide people to see things in a different way and that's really where the magic happens.

It's a different way of reacting, because the main message out there is, 'Don't stop hoping!' and I'm saying, 'Give up on hope!' I spent years with hope. It's almost a desperation, and there's a way in which holding onto that hope gets in the way of accepting and of opening up to what other possibilities might be available for you. Because you cling on; you're controlling everything, no stone is left unturned and you're trying to direct the course of life. Letting all that go is a scary thing to do. To let go like that you have to trust that it's going to be okay. Having a spiritual belief that maybe there's something bigger than you – a kind of larger perspective – is important. I know that has really made the difference for me and I am grateful for my journey that it helped me grow in that way.

I just love my coaching work. It energises me, because when I'm working with women I can see a change, or I can see the burden lessen, and it feeds my heart and soul that I'm able to offer that for someone else. It's amazing for me. Some of the stories I've heard really touch me. The lengths that some women have gone to – wow, it's amazing. Every single woman inspires me; everyone has this strength. They all just seem incredibly strong.

One of the things I remember from my session with the coach was when she asked me why I wanted to have children and I remember saying to her that I just had so much – it sounds a bit corny now – to give and love and I just wanted to create a family and love it. And she told me that there are so many ways to do that: so many ways to love or to create. Maybe Fertility Potentials does give me that opportunity – to share, and love and create.

Stella,

57, Lives in New Zealand

I'm from a big family: seven children, and I'm number five down the line. My eldest sibling had some problems that meant he was quite a handful, two of my other siblings had a difficult health condition and my Mum was working two days a week as well. So I felt a bit ambivalent about being a parent growing up, because it looked like a lot of hard work.

I was pretty determined to go my own way, and I felt like I didn't fit anywhere. As a teenager I went to boarding school but didn't last the distance. Then I went to a co-ed school that did skiing trips so I went skiing, and I immediately knew I wanted to find a way to do it more because it was so magical. I qualified as a chef even though I'm not a great cook. It was a means to an end for me – getting from place to place to ski. I travelled overseas for about three years, just making enough to get to the next place, and then came back to New Zealand and ended up living with a guy and working in Hawkes Bay for two years. It's a big winery area and people drank a lot of wine there.

I was probably drinking too much and that affected my decision-making. That relationship fell through, and I moved to Wellington and met another guy. I got pregnant, and there was somehow this expectation we were going to get married. He didn't really ask me so I never really asked myself; I just kind of went with it. As I said, I wasn't very good at making decisions for myself around then.

We had been taking the paint off the house; it was an old villa and I think it was lead paint and we weren't properly protecting ourselves. Maybe it was that – we also did a lot of drugs at that time as well so that might have played a part too – I'm not sure. But early in the pregnancy we found out that the baby had double the chromosomes it should have had and was never going to grow. I had to go into hospital and have it out. That brought me a lot of shame.

The following year I got pregnant again. I wasn't getting any counselling or any kind of support about what had happened with the first pregnancy, and things had gotten exponentially worse. My husband was going to go to rehab and I was pregnant. I knew we weren't in an ideal place to be having children. The day that he went to rehab was the same day I went in to have the first scan, and they said this child had also stopped growing, two weeks before. I had to go in and have it out, again.

That's when I made a decision to leave. I was 33, 34, and I thought, 'If I stay here I'm going to die. This isn't working, this is no good, I have to change my life.' The first pregnancy got me married, the second one got me unmarried.

I was so traumatised by what had happened I didn't get into a relationship again for three and a half years. I felt there was something wrong with me; I got pregnant and both times there was something wrong with the child. By then I really wanted to have a child but I felt a failure as a human being; if anyone knew me why would they want to have a child with me? I felt I was absolutely responsible for what had happened, and it woke me up to realise that I couldn't live like that, and it wasn't going to change unless I did something about it. I had a breakdown. But I did get clean and I've been clean ever since. That's 23 years now.

There were a couple of years after that where I just had to…I had nothing. Then I got a job in the film business which was very long hours, so there wasn't really any space to be in a relationship. It was just the most wonderful job – so good for me. I was there for five years and that put me in a position where I could buy a house. Things really started to turn around pretty dramatically. Things were good.

I was 36, 37 and I was very open to having children by then, but it wasn't going to happen if I was single. Friends encouraged me to start seeing men again and I got involved with a guy who was certainly a lot of fun, but he already had children and his one responsible act in life was to have had a vasectomy. At the beginning, when we got together, I said I still wanted to have children and he was like, 'Well, I can get it reversed!' A year down the track that changed to, 'I don't want to.' I had some counselling at that point, because I questioned myself about what was important to me and why I wanted to be a mother. I really struggled with it all, and eventually I thought I'd come to terms with it. I felt that if we weren't having children we needed to be doing something else, and buying a house together seemed like the right direction. I put up the money and we agreed to split the mortgage. But to cut a long story short it all fell over, very badly. We broke up, and one way or another he really did break my heart.

I had about a year and a half on my own after that, just thinking, 'Oh God I'm such a disaster!' Then my Dad died and I decided to go to art school. I had wanted to do that my whole life and I had been discouraged from doing so because it wasn't a proper career. 'But now,' I thought, 'I'm on my own. I don't have any…dependants. Why not?' I decided to sell the house, which I had renovated – it was like a sculptural project really, doing all of that – and my lawyer insisted I get a local builder to come and look at it before I put it on the market.

And when he – Gus, the builder – turned up…my response was immediate. I thought, 'Oh there you are!' It was so weird, like I already knew him. I was 44 then and he's ten years older than me. He's probably the most grown-up man I've ever met really. He's very sensitive and he answers something in me that I must have missed out on, and I think I do for him as well. And at 46 – 46! – I got pregnant to him.

It was so unexpected; I didn't think I could. I thought I'd already left all that behind. It was like a miracle. He wasn't so excited because he'd just had his first grandchild, but the very day that he came around to say, 'Even though it's not quite what I wanted, I love you, and I'm up for it,' I went in for a scan and again...the baby had died. It was just heartbreaking, because it had seemed so miraculous.

I left; it was just too much. I didn't leave straight away. I was living in town and going out to Gus's in the weekends so superficially everything was still okay, and I finished my Arts degree. But it was all just too hard. I decided to go to Australia and do my Masters there. Gus and I had a long-distance relationship the first year or so but then I broke up with him – not because I didn't like him but because I couldn't...I didn't know what to do with him. I was in Australia a few years, but it wasn't working out. I didn't fit there either.

I think what happened is the grief; I sort of went back into abdicating any responsibility for myself and I got quite isolated as well. I think I was pretty depressed actually, and just not able to make decisions or take action. I knew I was in trouble but I couldn't help myself.

Then in September 2010, while I was still in Sydney, the first big earthquake happened back in Christchurch and Gus began to work there, travelling down from Hawkes Bay, three weeks on and one week off. He was about two weeks away from finishing completely when the even bigger February earthquake happened. He was there, in Christchurch, when it hit, and he called me in total shock. It was that earthquake that brought us back together, because I immediately thought, 'What if something had happened to him!' He visited me in Australia to get a break from the ongoing earthquakes and destruction in Christchurch, and he saw I was getting myself into trouble. I was basically spending my money without replenishing it, and I'd sort of got stuck. Eventually he said, 'Why don't you come to Christchurch? Just come for six months or a year. There's no obligation; you don't need to stay, just come for a little while and get your breath back.' Christchurch! That wasn't quite on my game plan! But it was very open ended so that's why I came here, and it's been the best thing. He's given me the space just to be able to heal, and he's never ignored the fact that we share my loss.

I've since done some therapeutic Family Constellation work about those pregnancy losses. That really reconnected me with my children, and as a result of that I named them: Serena, Poppy and Charlie. Charlie would be 12 and the other two would be 23 and 24. I'm finding my way now through their presence – and their absence – in my life. Since doing that work I feel their presence more, and in fact my work got much more playful after that. I think the sadness gave me a bad case of terminal seriousness or something; the joy had gone out of things!

Being in Christchurch has been very good to me. Coming here it seemed rude to be feeling sorry for myself when so many people are traumatised through no fault of their own because of the earthquakes. I realised I needed to get my head out of my arse and do something useful, and it's actually changed my art practice considerably being here. It got me thinking about how art can be useful for healing in a situation like this.

And making my work is so important to me; having that creative life is essential I think. I can't imagine how I would live without it, because if I didn't have that, well I'm not being melodramatic when I say I actually feel there would be absolutely no point to me. This is what I can do.

Vicki,

44, Lives in New Zealand

Life has just been on pause for the past six years really. Maybe there is some other reason why I'm on this earth, something else that I'm supposed to do with my energy. I feel like I'm just right at the beginning of the journey of figuring out what else is possible and how I can lead a meaningful and fulfilling life. I'm starting to come out of the haze a little bit.

The last few years have been the hardest of my life, but it's getting better. There was a phase that a day wouldn't go by where I didn't cry my eyes out. Birthdays were always triggers; 39 is the last birthday I can remember really celebrating. Since then my birthdays have just been really dark periods. Another nail in the coffin.

I always thought I could have kids, I never questioned it. It was what I wanted, and I remember even as a teenager having quite active fantasies about motherhood and the daughter I thought I'd have. I was always juggling names; I still do some days, and I catch myself and go, 'What are you doing that for?' I still hear a name and…try it on for size.

I actually did get pregnant when I was 22 and I had an abortion. It was never about not wanting kids; it was that I felt like I'd done something so wrong. I'd done the thing my family always warned me about, and I was so full of fear and shame. I just couldn't tell them. I never knew that that would be my only pregnancy, never imagined that was my only chance. I was part of a generation of women who grew up being told that the worst thing we could do would be to get ourselves pregnant, and that message was so instilled in me that I spent most of my most fertile years terrified of getting pregnant and doing everything I could to not to. Not once did anybody ever tell me that it would be okay. Now I meet women who had their kids at a young age unexpectedly, and things worked out for them.

I thought about that child for a long time, though it's less present now.

I remember when I turned 30 being worried about the fact that I was single and I wanted to have a family, and that anxiety got more intense around my mid-30s. I met my current partner when I was 37 and he was 44, and we discussed really early on – I think probably within the first few weeks that we were together – that we both wanted kids. About a year into our relationship we started trying; I was 38. That was six years ago now and it hasn't happened for us. We went through all the fertility tests, and I remember being told quite categorically by one consultant that we saw – I think I was 39 at the time – that at my age I had a 16 per cent chance of conceiving. She was very bleak about it.

I'm very into organic healthy living so I went down that route. I went to acupuncture, and cranial osteopathy, and naturopathy, and even hypnotherapy at one point; I thought it was maybe a deep-seated psychological issue that was blocking us from having a baby. Nothing. I decided not to do IVF, because everything in my being said 'no' to that somehow. I always believed it was going to happen naturally. Those years were a long cycle of hope and disappointment, hope and disappointment. And shame and grief and hopelessness. There were some really dark days where I literally couldn't see a future for myself.

But in this last year I've made a conscious choice to face into the stark reality that if it hasn't happened in six years, then the likelihood that it happens now at 44 is pretty small. I'm not sure exactly what made it possible to make that final decision, but now I'm trying to find some acceptance. For the first time in a long time I can see other possibilities, and I can start to feel excited about things in my future. I practise a lot of yoga and meditation, and that's been really helpful for me. I remember hearing a yoga teacher – who had gone through this herself actually – saying that yoga doesn't have the answers to your situation, but it can teach you a lot about letting go and acceptance.

Acceptance means feeling all of the grief and the rage fully. It's been a long piece of work and I felt very hypocritical at times because in my work I'd be talking to my clients about acceptance, but refusing to do it in my own life. But practising acceptance has helped a lot. I have these little affirmation cards and there's one that says, 'The moment you accept the troubles you have been given, the door will open.' For about a year I had that on my bookcase and was reading it every day.

I think the other thing that helps is just reminding myself that people have much worse things than this in life that they have to confront and accept. I mean there are women out there who have kids and then lose them, and I can't even begin to conceive of what they go through. It helps to know that everybody has their struggle in life and this one happens to be mine.

It's been a really hard few years for friendships because my friends have just been popping out the babies left right and centre, and it's really tested my relationships with quite a few people. It's hard to be happy for them; I've had moments of intense rage. But I've softened a little bit now. I have more of a recognition that everybody else is on their own path and it's got nothing to do with mine.

Hope is quite toxic. People still say to me, 'Oh I haven't given up hope for you!' and I get really mad because I just don't want to be stuck in that cycle anymore. Hope keeps you stuck in non-acceptance; it keeps you stuck in the fantasy that things are going to be different. It's such an unhealthy way to live; it takes you completely out of your real life. My relationship with my partner has suffered, my relationship with my friends has suffered, my relationship with myself has suffered, and all my energy has gone into this thing that's not happening.

I think it's been a different journey for my partner. When I met him he was 44 and, although he would love to have kids and he would be an awesome father, I think he'd already made his peace with the fact that that might not happen. I don't think he's struggled with it in the same way that I have, and it created a lot of distance between us. There was a period where I would just be crying every day and it got to the point – and he's a psychotherapist so he's not an insensitive guy – where he would see me crying on the couch and just carry on about his business and not even acknowledge it. Because it was just all the time and I don't think he knew what to do with me anymore. Now I feel like I'm emerging from this haze and trying to repair the damage it has done to our relationship. Not that we're in a terrible place, but I feel like I've neglected the relationship quite a lot through this process and withdrawn from him – from everyone! – because I just felt like nobody could understand me.

For a long time I imagined that the grief would just get even worse, that next would come menopause and that would be catastrophic, and then it would be getting older and not having family. But now I can actually see that maybe it can also be a relief – that this phase is finally over and I can stop thinking about it. I like to think that we all have some gift to share with the world and it's finding out what that is. Something that feels like it's what I was put here for. I don't know yet what form that's going to take, but I'm starting to recognise that I don't want to identify myself for the rest of my life as a childless woman. I want to be something else.

Natasha,

55, Lives in England

My mother did two interesting things when I was growing up: she didn't let me learn typing at school because she was a secretary and she didn't want me to do that, and she didn't let me learn how to sew or use a sewing machine because my family were immigrants who had set up factories for making clothes. She wanted more for me. I was academic and very bright, and I managed to get into Cambridge – the first person from my family to go to university and the first from my school to go there – and it was a very big deal. I was one of the first intake of women to an all-male Cambridge college: 400 men and 36 women undergraduates. My mother remains incredulous that I didn't manage to find myself a husband with those odds, but no, I did not.

I think, given a free rein, I would have studied English or History, which were my two passions, but it was the 1970s. There was a three-day week, strikes and power cuts and everything looked really dire. My parents said, 'You've got an opportunity to go to university; for God's sake go and learn something useful like law where it leads into a profession. You can always read books.' So I read law and it was not that easy for me. I wasn't particularly fired up about being a lawyer.

I had a number of boyfriends during my Cambridge years, but nothing serious. After law school, I did my training at a law firm in London and during that period I met somebody and got married. Looking back I see that I married for all the wrong reasons, and even that I knew it at the time, but I really liked his family. Sometimes I say I fell in love with his family. I remember the day that I finally left our home; my husband's father rang me to say, 'I hope you know that you are divorcing our son, not us.' I was 33 at the time and his family is still part of my life.

In my mid 20s – around the time I met my husband – I was diagnosed with polycystic-ovary syndrome and endometriosis. I remember my gynaecologist telling me that if I wanted to have children I'd better get on with it. So we were getting on with it. And then I somehow managed to throw a bomb into my life; I changed law firm, met somebody and fell in love with him. He was married, I was married; my marriage ended, his marriage ended and it was an absolute mess. The relationship with him didn't survive either. It took me a very, very long time to cope with that double loss. I wouldn't have seen it at that stage as grief, but it was. I was in a job that I didn't like at the time, so I thought I'd take a break, get away from London and go travelling. I was about 38, 39 by this time. I had a fantastic time – I'll never regret doing that – and then I came back and realised my 40s were hurtling towards me. I started to get really, really scared about the possibility of never having a child.

The absolute cut-off date in my head was 45, so as I turned 40 I was absolutely desperate to meet someone and make it stick, and have a family. Looking back now, I see I was in a bubble of denial because, given my gynaecological history – there were cysts, problems with the endometriosis and fibroids – my moment had probably already completely passed, but in my head I still had some time. I thought of having a child on my own, but I knew people who had gone down the single-mother route and I just felt that wasn't for me. I have a history of depression and anxiety, and I thought: 'What the hell happens if I can't cope? Who will be there for the child?'

So I basically asked every person I knew, 'Do you know anyone you can introduce me to?' I had some American friends who said, 'We know somebody. We know this guy who's just moved to London. Why don't we have a Thanksgiving dinner and invite loads of people. We'll sit you next to him, and see if something happens!' And that's how I met Mark.

I was 42 by then, desperate to have a child, desperate to make a family. Mark was superficially an amazing guy and I was absolutely blown away by him. It lasted on and off for six years and during that time I realised that he was intrinsically deceitful and unfaithful. He could never actually be with someone without having an affair with somebody else on the side. It was a complete nightmare, but I couldn't let it go because I thought, 'I've got to make this work; it's my very last chance to have a child.'

At 44 – in the middle of this maelstrom – I spontaneously fell pregnant, which was a complete miracle. Even my gynaecologist said she couldn't believe it. Mark was stunned and shocked, but in a bad way. He didn't want it.

I had a miscarriage at just three months. It was really heartbreaking and I was absolutely crazy to try again. I had a fantasy about how it would be to have a family; I had names for my children ready. I was desperate to have IVF and dragged Mark along to an IVF specialist. I don't know why he went really, because the day before we were meant to be starting the programme he told me that he didn't want to do it and the relationship was over. It was a really strange time because it was the night before the London bombing on 7 July 2007, and I was at his flat. We had this awful row and I walked out. Had I not, I might have been on one of the tubes that were affected. Looking back, I know I didn't lose my life or my limbs, but I did lose something huge. The dream of being a mother was over.

I fell into a really, really deep depression. I'd had bouts of depression from when I was a teenager, but those were like a flirtation with depression. This was the real deal. I didn't realise I could ever get so low; it was just absolutely awful. There was a double loss: of the relationship and of ever being a mother, but the mother piece was by far the hardest to bear.

When I hit my grief about my childlessness I didn't even know it was grief. Meeting Jody Day and coming across

Gateway Women have been a huge part of my recovery. I read her book and I thought, 'Oh my God, this is grief! I'm completely stuck in depression because I'm not actively grieving.' I joined a Gateway Women programme that Jody was running with a group of ten women, and over a period of two years I did intensive one-to-one work with her as well.

I did a lot of deep thinking about what it is to actively grieve and what I needed to do. Childlessness is a grief that's not recognised societally. What are you grieving for? You haven't lost a child. Yes, I could say I'm grieving my miscarriage and people would recognise that's a tangible loss; that makes sense. But childlessness itself is such an *int*angible loss; I never got to be a mother. I can be okay saying that now, but at the time I was in this terrible dark, dead place and full of shame as well. I didn't talk about it to anyone. I couldn't talk about it to my parents, I couldn't talk about it to my friends; it was absolutely horrendous.

It hit me like a punch in my stomach any time people brought babies into the office, or there were birth announcements, or if I heard that anyone was pregnant. I just couldn't bear it. And I'm from a Jewish family; the thing we do is marry and have a family. I felt terribly guilty that I'd let my parents down and let myself down. I had all this time to make it happen and I hadn't been able to, and what the fuck was wrong with me? For a long time I thought I was a complete failure because I hadn't had a child, and nothing, absolutely nothing else in life was worthwhile.

It took me about three years to work my way through and

out of my grief. I can't pinpoint the moment I was clear of it, but suddenly I was. Things started to change when I realised that I wasn't alone, that there were lots of women going through this. Before that I had felt really isolated; even though I could look around my life and identify quite a lot of women who didn't have children, we'd never had a conversation about it. It was if we were all gagged by our shame. Now I'm much more relaxed about talking about it because I feel part of a tribe of women supporting each other as they grieve and recover.

The way I describe my life now is that I am fully embracing a sense of agency. A sense of competency, of being really on top of my game. For a long time I felt I was a complete fake as a lawyer and any moment I was going to be found out. Now I don't. I actually think I'm bloody good at my job. In the area of law in which I specialise, I'm one of the top lawyers in the world. It's amazing to me that I'm actually saying that.

When I stopped being depressed and came out the other side of my grief, all the negative-shit seemed to fall away and there was this great release of energy. I thought, 'Well, okay, I'm in my 50s. What am I going to do with this energy? With the rest of my life?' There were lots of false starts, bouncing around ideas, trying things out. And then things just started to coalesce and to come together. I would try something new and think, 'Oh that feels good, that works for me,' or, 'That doesn't,' and now I've got this massive list of things that I want to do. I feel so much better now in my mid-50s than I ever did at 35 or 25 and definitely 45. I never thought I would feel this way. Life is constantly surprising me.

I have energy to take on new things. I'm a director of two social enterprise companies, one looking into the impact of ageing without children. I've co-founded another. I've joined the Liberal Democrats, I'm politically canvassing. I'm doing things that I would never have believed that I would have the confidence let alone energy to do. I just feel like...I don't know how to describe it. I feel like I'm in my power!

It's actually a miraculous thing to be able to say this. Five years ago, I was in such a dark place. And if anyone had told me that I would ever feel this positive again about my life, about myself, I would have said, 'That's just not going to happen.'

How did it happen? I came to realise that I'd had a negative, distorted and very, very unpleasantly vitriolic and brutal self-critic. One of the really big ameliorating factors was self-compassion. When I challenged that critical inner voice and started to think about my experience and what had happened to me, I realised that I had tried to do the best that I could at every stage of my life. Instead of berating and castigating and punishing myself for failing, I started to feel a heartfelt sense of compassion for myself and my struggle, how it just hadn't been possible for me to do everything and achieve everything I'd wanted. And in doing that self-compassion work, the daily practice of it, over a period of time, I went way past just getting to the point of feeling okay. I transformed myself. It's really like a miracle.

Feeling compassion for yourself is very different to feeling sorry for yourself. That's self-pity and it's quite a negative loop. It's poor me. I think self-compassion is about seeing our struggle as a very human experience that connects us all. Everyone struggles in their life. For a woman – whether you're a mother or you don't manage to have children – you have your path, and there will be struggle and pain as well as success and joy. I started to look at my friends with children and some of them were having very difficult experiences. And I thought, 'No one gets an idyllic life. To be human comes at this cost of pain and sorrow, and everyone has that. My pain and suffering, which is around not having a child and not having a family, is just one form of suffering of many, many forms. There's no hierarchy of suffering.' I found that thought sobering but comforting. We are all in this shit and wonder together.

If my depression and grief were my darkness, I'm in my light now. I'm seeing that there is meaning and joy in life that actually doesn't involve a man and a child. Most of my life I thought that my happiness would be totally tied up in those two things. I'm dating again, but in such a different way, because I'm not looking for the father of my child; I'm not even looking for someone to make my life complete. I'm not looking for someone to do my DIY or my finances. I'm looking for a companion, and it's a completely different thing. And you know what? If I don't meet someone, that's okay. I'm still going to have a great life!

Having said all that, I feel you never completely heal. It's always there, the loss, but you heal around your pain and sadness. It becomes part of who you are. Being childless doesn't have to mean stagnating in your darkness. It is possible to move through and past the darkness into a different life.

It's strange that you can hold those seemingly two contra-dictory things: the fact that you would still prefer to have had children, but you can still have a rich life.

It's been such an amazing process. I still don't know where it's going!

About the Author

Dr Lois Tonkin has worked as a counsellor, educator and writer about issues of loss and grieving for over 25 years. She has a special interest in the disenfranchised grief experienced by people who have non-bereavement losses. She is well known in the UK and New Zealand for her work about the ways people 'grow around grief', where they find ways to 'live with' their losses rather than 'get over' them.

Lois is a lecturer in counselling and in qualitative research methods at the University of Canterbury/Te Whare Wānanga o Waitaha, New Zealand. She is also a counsellor for Genea Oxford Fertility in Christchurch. She lives in Diamond Harbour, Aotearoa/New Zealand.

Index

abortion 31–2, 48–9, 70, 98–9, 103,
 134–5, 153, 204
 medical 197
 and right to have children 100
 shame 137
acceptance 74, 193, 205–6
acupuncture 74
adaptation 28
adoption 52–4, 77–8, 84, 95, 101
 from another country 185–7
 attitudes to 184–5
 experience of 75
adulthood, parenting as 140
affirmation 205–6
age 42, 46, 47, 53, 59
 death and dying 117–18
 and fertility 140–1
 and loss of possibility 130–1
 risks of 141
agency 213
alcohol 160, 196–7
alternative therapies 205
ambitions, achieving 199
ambivalence 47, 102, 119, 134
anger 22

anomaly, feeling 149
anxiety 175, 177, 204, 210
 and adoption 53–4
artificial insemination 36–7
assumptions 50, 143
attitudes
 to childlessness 28–9, 32–3
 of other women 50
aunts, role as 50, 60–1, 132
author experiences 23–4

Baby Maddas 134
back-up parenting 38
beauty, of pregnancy 39
belief 69, 191
 and expectation 72
 spiritual 71
belonging 34, 150–1
bereavement 42, 109, 135, 199
biochemical pregnancy 165
biological clock 87, 103, 123–4, 140–1,
 209–10
biology, pressure of 84
birthdays, sadness of 203
blame 27, 54, 121

bodies
  commonalities of 92
  and feelings 92
  taking care of 163
book
  aims 28–9
  background 21–4
  development of 25–6
  questions 24
  storytelling/retelling 25–6

camaraderie 50
careers 42, 45, 50, 70–1, 89
  as caring 194–5
  creativity 201–2
  dominance 74
  effect of childlessness 162
  as expressions of maternal feelings
      89, 111–14, 154–5, 175, 176
  as priority 76–7, 83, 95–6, 98, 153
  as self-expression 131
  and self-image 213
  as turnaround 198
  see also work
carers 60
caring
  alternatives 175
  for children 38
change, making 198
childfree, vs. childless 24, 107, 161, 184
childhood
  attitudes 46
  influence of 150–2
childlessness
  opportunities of 22, 28, 84, 192–3
  understanding 121–2
children
  being around 99–100
  delight in 92–3
  parent/carer reactions to 30

child's perspective 181
choice making 23, 86, 157
  different 149
  implications of 60, 181
  limits of 48–59, 103, 104
  motivations for 57–8
Christchurch earthquake 200–1
Christmas, difficulties of 132
co-parenting 46–7
comfort eating 101
commonalities
  of bodies 92
  of parenthood 146–7
competency 213
conception, dominance of 192
consistency, of desire for a child 59–60
counselling 48, 50, 111, 198–9
creativity
  expressions of 194–5, 201–2
  of motherhood 47–8
curiosity 33–4, 50

dating 198–9
  purpose of 215
  and wanting children 123
Day, J. 121, 137, 156, 211–12
decision making
  circumstances of 24–5
  factors in 58–9
  implications of 60
  and regret 103
depression 47, 87–8, 117–18, 177, 200,
    210, 211
deserving 137
destiny 150
disabilities, risk of 141
distress 21, 174–5
divorce 145
  experience of 41–2
Dreaming of a Life Unlived (John) 138

dreams 55–6, 178
  letting go of 192
  loss of 211
drinking, alcohol 160, 196–7
drug use 197

education 42, 91, 117
egg freezing 125–6, 163–4
emotional support 33
endometriosis 185, 191, 209, 210
energy 213–14
  for parenting 187
  use of 84
envy 159
ethics 118
excitement 22
exclusion 149
existential crisis 122
expectations 69, 72, 73–4, 102, 108, 162,
    173, 203
experiences
  in common 21
  missed 47–8, 54–5, 106

facing reality 205
failure, fear of 59–60
falling in love 30–1
family
  cultural importance 164
  culture of 99–100
  desire for 34, 47–8, 74
  and heritage 124
  influence of 128–9, 134, 191, 196
  nature of 66
  sense of 146
Family Constellation 201
fantasies 203
fathers
  relationships with 169, 179–80
  role of 178

fear 130, 151, 152, 169
  of pregnancy 204
feeling ready 64
feminism 30, 31, 102, 117, 128
fertility 72, 124–5
fertility testing 136, 204
fertility treatment 184
financial considerations 65, 164, 170–1,
    175
fitting in 196
footprint 50–1
forgiveness 27, 104, 137
fostering 77–9, 101, 112–13
freedom
  of childlessness 50
  motherhood as loss of 73–4
friendships
  and involvement with children 60–1
  maintaining 61
  strain on 206
fulfilment 96–7
future
  hope for 34
  optimism 51
  thoughts for 22, 40

Gateway Women 121, 137, 156, 211–12
geography 150–1
godchildren 34
grandchildren 35, 189
grief 27, 38, 47, 48, 104, 106, 112, 121, 130,
    131, 148, 185, 190, 200, 211–12
  burden of 207
  coming to terms with 131–2
  intensity of 137, 203
  legitimacy of 100
  as long process 142–3
  managing 137–8
  recognition of 158
  working through 193, 212–13

guarantees 172–3
guilt 21, 212
gynaecological problems 52–3

healing 104–5, 160, 215–16
health 47, 177, 191, 205, 209–10
helping others 193–4
heritage 124
homestay students 79–81
hope 175
    for future 34
    letting go 194
    as toxic 28, 206
hopelessness 31–2
husbands, feelings 136
    see also men

identity 60
imagining 69, 85, 93, 120, 142, 166,
    187–8
independence 169, 172, 196
infertility 26
    effect on relationships 184–5
infidelity 33
invisibility 22
isolation 33, 193, 213
IVF 42–3, 44, 52–3, 72–3, 74, 83, 84,
    165–6, 190, 205, 211

Jackie 21
journey 192–3
joy 94, 215
    loss of 192, 201
Judaism 212
judgement, sense of 106, 143

kinship 61
Koyaanisqatsi 83

learning, reciprocal 62
legacy 42, 62, 147
legislation 122
lesbian culture 31, 36–7, 181–2
'Let go and let God' approach 127
letter to an unborn child 138–9
letting go 192
    of hope 194
life
    creation of 131
    pausing 203
    pausing and restarting 191
    restructuring 59
    shrinking 158–9
life histories 25
liminality 44
limits of possibility 42
living in-the-moment 46
'Living without children' workshop 137
loneliness 172, 176, 193
loss 22, 27, 39–40, 49, 62, 85, 106–7, 112,
    129, 142, 148, 165, 190–1, 215–16
    intangible 212
love 129
    capacity for 62
    expressions of 194–5
    giving 81
    loss of 106–7
    mother as 69

marginalisation 106
marriage 135–6, 153–4, 197–8
    as aspiration 108
    breakdown 209
    choices and decisions in 32, 47
    reasons for 209
masculine environments 91
maternal feelings 111–12
    lessening 176

meaning 122, 215
media representations 122
meditation 74, 160, 192, 205
men
    attitudes/feelings 32, 46, 47, 52–3, 65,
        67, 70, 136
    circumstantial childlessness 27
menopause 63, 77, 105, 153–4, 166, 187,
    207
mental health
    anxiety 53–4, 177, 210
    breakdown 198
    depression 47, 87–8, 117–18, 177, 200,
        210, 211
messages, to women 44–5
miscarriage 37, 76–7, 119–20, 190, 211
missing out 118–19, 142, 160, 176–7, 188
mixed feelings 33
morality 118
mortality 79
mother-child relationship 33–4
motherhood
    as caring 105
    as creative 47–8
    expectations of 73–4
    hopes for 21
    as love 69
    meaning of 100, 154–5
    as meant/not meant 88–9
    as need 87–8
    as opportunity 54–5
    as perilous 102–3
    as purpose 83–4
    as self-image 141
    ubiquity of 158
mothering
    alternatives 24, 28, 60–1, 79–81, 89,
        96–7, 101, 154–5
    social context of 24–5

mothers
    death of 42
    relationships with 168–9
        see also parent/carer influence
Mother's Day 66
moving on 215–16

names 142
    choosing 73
    juggling 203
    see also imagining
naming, of lost children 201
needs
    fulfilling 34
    motherhood as 87–8
new things, trying 213–14
New Year, difficulties of 132
not knowing 63
nurturing 100–1, 112, 129, 141–2, 143–4
nutrition 74

online dating 119
opportunities 22, 28, 84, 192–3, 213
optimism 51
options
    as childless woman 131
    for motherhood 89
Organisation for Economic Co-
    operation and Development
    (OECD) 23
ovarian reserve 124–5

parent/carer abuse 151–2
parent/carer influence 30, 41, 69–70,
    150, 152, 162, 168, 174–6, 178–81,
    208–9
parent/child relationship 129
parenthood, commonalities of 146–7

parenting
  as adulthood 140
  as distinct from having a baby 182
  joy of 94
  part-time 38
partners, impact on 206–7
pathologisation 24
peace 88, 89–90, 193
perfection, looking for 157
perimenopause 71
personal growth 142–3, 192–3, 213–14
pets 171
pity 84–5
'Plan B Mentorship programme' 137
planning/not planning 57
policy 122
polycystic-ovary syndrome 209, 210
positivity 126–7
possibilities
  alternatives 205
  limits of 42
post-traumatic stress disorder (PTSD)
  109–11
pragmatism 67–8, 130, 187
pregnancy 98, 119–20, 199–200
  ambivalence 65
  attempts 36
  beauty of 39
  biochemical 165
  excitement of 190
  as potential 62–3
  testing for/identifying 82–3
pretence 147
procrastination 176
procreation instinct 158
promiscuity 174
pseudonyms, use of 26
psychosocial context 25
purpose 83–4, 122, 172, 203

rainbow analogy 55–6
re-programming 191
realisation 156
reality, facing 205
recognition 39, 66–7, 122, 212
regret 31–2, 106, 172
  of earlier decisions 103
  fear of 22, 34–5, 177
  limits of possibility 42
  as pointless 41
relationships 31, 36–7, 46, 52, 65, 70, 76,
  119, 198–200, 204
  bad 210–11
  breaking up 58
  effect of infertility 184–5
  finding the right man 145–6
  long-distance 199–200
  with men in and out of family 174
  motherhood and love of partner
    47–8, 67–8
  with mothers 168–9
  with parents 129
  proxying 62
  re-starting 200–1
  testing 206–7
relief 28
religion 135
resignation 33
resilience 83
responses, dealing with 105–6
rights 122
rituals, for healing 104–5

sadness 22, 34, 85, 93, 99–100, 136,
  187–8
  for partner 193
school 91
self awareness 100–1
self-compassionate attitude 122, 214–15

self-criticism 214
self-esteem 45
self-image 59, 184
self-knowledge 31
self-ownership 153–4
self-pity 214
self-protection 147
self-reliance 130
selfishness 171–2
    sense of 31
selflessness 33–4
sense making 74
sex work 179
sexual abuse 151–2
sexual orientation 30–1, 36–7
sexualisation 174
sexuality, accepting 181–2
shame 137, 204, 212, 213
sharing experience 193–4
silence, social 28–9
single parenting 46–7, 64–5, 123, 164–5,
    175, 185–6
    child's experience 69–70
    fear and shame 204
skiing 196
social silence 28–9, 148
social structures, effects on 24
socio-political context 122
sperm donation 36–7, 164–5, 166
spirituality 71, 72–3
statistics 22–3
stepchildren 65–7, 93–4, 145–6, 189
stillbirth 43–4
stress 175

suffering 215
sustainability 51

talking 143, 149, 193–4, 213
    about feelings 49–50, 159–60
    importance of 122
terminations see abortion
thankfulness 67
therapy 41, 88, 118, 119, 129
time 70–1
timing 170
traditions, passing on 124
trans perspective 91–7
transitioning 95
trauma 108–11, 151–2, 198
trust 152–3

uncertainty 63, 86
university 208–9

wanting what you can't have 157
weight 101
whakapapa 164
what ifs 59–60, 104
    emotional support 61–2
work 89
    as expression of maternal feelings
        194–5
    see also careers
worries 73–4
wounded healer 155

yoga 205